# JUMPSTART
## *your*
# PRODUCTIVITY

## —10 JOLTS—
### TO GET AND STAY
### MASSIVELY PRODUCTIVE

# SHAWN DOYLE CSP

# DEDICATION

With Love—
To my extraordinary parents, Jack and Sue Doyle who taught me
to believe that all things are possible.

SOUND WISDOM
P.O. Box 310
Shippensburg, PA 17257-0310

For more information on publishing and distribution rights, call 717-530-2122 or info@soundwisdom.com

**Quantity Sales.** Special discounts are available on quantity purchases by corporations, associations, and others. For details, contact the Sales Department at Sound Wisdom.

While efforts have been made to verify information contained in this publication, neither the author nor the publisher assumes any responsibility for errors, inaccuracies, or omissions.

While this publication is chock-full of useful, practical information; it is not intended to be legal or accounting advice. All readers are advised to seek competent lawyers and accountants to follow laws and regulations that may apply to specific situations.

The reader of this publication assumes responsibility for the use of the information. The author and publisher assume no responsibility or liability whatsoever on the behalf of the reader of this publication.

ISBN 13 TP: 978-1-937879-56-3
ISBN 13 eBook: 978-1-937879-57-0

For Worldwide Distribution, Printed in the U.S.A.
2 3 4 5 6 7 8 / 20 19 18 17

Cover/Jacket design: Eileen Rockwell
Interior design: Terry Clifton

# CONTENTS

# INTRODUCTION

Hello and welcome to *Jumpstart Your Productivity*. My name is Shawn Doyle, and I am a professional speaker, book author, executive coach, and consultant. I have a very successful company, and that means I am extremely busy, so I have to focus on how to be the most productive every day and every week (sometimes every hour). Think of me as your trusted tour guide into the world of better productivity.

I have a confession to make—I am endlessly fascinated by the topic of productivity. As I travel around the country speaking and training and consulting, one of the biggest stressors that I see in many people is managing their time, and not being able to get everything done that they need to get done in the time they have available. They just aren't as productive as they would like to be. People lead very busy lives personally and professionally. *Is that you?* Do you feel like at the end of the week you have run out of week and are not able to get everything done on your list?

Are you frustrated? Are you in an endless cycle of working super hard, but just not getting it all done? Do you feel like the circus performer who spins all the plates, and you don't want a plate to get dropped and smash on the floor? Do some of the plates fall and crash anyway? Well my friend, you are not alone. There are many people just like you suffering from the same challenges around productivity.

Yes, that is right—it seems to me that many people are in the crazy plate-smashing circus. People seem to be stressed out, overworked, not as productive as they want to be, and massively frustrated that they're not able to be productive. People are not just overwhelmed, but massively overwhelmed times ten! Many of the executives that I coach tell me that they need to work more on having work-life balance because they are spending a lot more time at work than they are with their family. They need to figure out how to be more productive while at the same time having more work-life balance. The demands on their time and their workloads are not less, but more.

It is my sincere hope that I will be able to bring you, in this book, some tools and ideas and techniques that will help make your life easier, yet more effective and productive. Along the way, I will also share with you some stories, examples, and ideas and add in some fun as well. Because, after all, productivity can be fun—right?

## CAUTIONS ABOUT PRODUCTIVITY

When we talk about productivity, there are a few things that I would like you to think about first.

Here are eight ideas that I would like you to consider in relation to productivity.

1.   **When I talk about productivity, I don't mean you should *work harder or longer* hours**. I mean actually the opposite—that I want you to work less hard, and fewer hours. Some people call this working smart. To me, being truly productive means being able to do more in less time, which will free you up to do other things in your life that you're just not getting to. I want you to learn to work lean and mean, and become a productivity machine.

2.   **When I talk about productivity, I also think productivity should include a discussion about what you should get rid of and eliminate in your daily activities.** To me, far too many people are in a state of overwhelm because they are trying to do too much within the amount of time they have available. They also suffer from what I refer to as the "superhero syndrome," meaning that they think they can get it all done. Well, guess what? You don't have a cape, you don't have a costume, and as much as you'd like to have one, you don't have a sidekick (okay, maybe you have a husband or wife who could probably be your sidekick); after all, every Batman needs a Robin, and every quarterback needs a receiver, and every Mickey needs a Minnie. So part of productivity also includes making more thoughtful decisions about what you're able to do and learning to just say no. I also think that an additional impediment to productivity, aside from having too many tasks to do, is having too many things to keep track of. The more things we have to keep track of, organize, maintain, sort, file, and so on, the more time we have to spend doing that and the less time we can spend being truly productive.

3.   **I don't think you have to be some sort of genius or guru in order to be massively productive.** I think what it really takes is to start being more consciously aware of how you spend your time and your efforts and analyzing whether you're spending them

effectively. You need to become a little bit of a productivity geek and think about how you can hack your productivity. I also think you have to be able to clearly articulate what your goals are. The number of people in the world who do not have clearly articulated goals is, unfortunately, shockingly low. In my opinion, far too many people are living their life flying by the seat of their pants. When I ask people what their plan is or what their goals are, they tend to give me a blank look as if I asked them what planet they are from. (The answer is Earth, by the way—I hope I didn't offend anyone on Mars.)

4. **I don't think there is a perfect textbook definition of productivity.** It is going to be up to you to decide exactly what that means for you, for your life, and for your world. It would not make any sense for me to try to impose my definition of productivity on you. I have always written about and thought that you are the architect of your own life, so it will be entirely up to you how you apply the concepts outlined here. As you read through the book and identify the tools and tips, the techniques, my only request is that you actually try them, to see if they will change your level of productivity for your life. After all, there is something that motivated you to read this book and it is probably because you're not currently satisfied with your level of productivity, and you are hoping that this book will help.

5. **Don't get too caught up in the terminology of productivity.** I think we can talk about productivity and time management at the same time. People talk at the same time about being more organized. In fact, when I teach these concepts to my clients, I often find that people get a little mixed up between time management and productivity and organization. I do not, however, think they are the same thing. I think that managing your time helps you

to be more productive. I think that being more organized helps you to be more productive. I don't think productivity is time management at all—productivity is so much more. Time management is only one piece of being more productive. So time management and organization skills are some tools to help you *become more productive.*

6.  **I don't expect you to embrace or agree with everything I suggest about being more productive.** Feel free to disagree. In fact, I think it is a sign of a healthy mind if you disagree with some of the concepts that I bring up. To me, in order to become more productive, you need to 1) use your life experience, background, and intelligence, combined with 2) reading other productivity books (yes, I know that you're cheating on me reading other productivity books), as well as 3) training and advice you've gotten from others along the way, 4) using systems and processes. I'm just asking you to consider some of the tools and techniques and to try to see if they will work for you—if they do, great; if they don't, feel free to jettison them along the roadside and continue your life's journey. But I guarantee you that you will want to have some of them packed to take with you because they will be valuable tools for you to use.

7.  **I want you to *think about how you think* in regard to productivity.** Many people that I meet seem to have preconceived notions about themselves in regard to productivity. They will say, "Well, you know I'm not very productive—because I'm a little too scattered." Or they will say, "I just have never really been a very productive person." People give me an endless list of *negative statements* about their abilities to be productive. The reason I want you to be aware of what it is that you're saying to yourself is because it can also become a form of acceptance. If someone has really

negative thoughts, they become a self-fulfilling prophecy. What I want you to think instead is "I would like to become more productive, and I'm capable of becoming more productive and doing the work to be that way." Some people ask me, "Aren't some people just born more productive and more organized?" Here is what I believe: there are some people who were just born with a little more of the productive gene, and they tend to be that way their whole life. However, I think most people are the exception to that rule. Most people that I meet are willing to learn, so they figured out along the way how to be more productive through reading and studying and training. So the good news is that productivity is a *learned skill*. It's not some sort of voodoo magic. Yes, you can learn it. What I want you to reflect on as we go through this journey together is how you can modify your thinking about productivity. Instead of creating a negative expectation by saying that you're not productive, say to yourself that you can be more productive and that you just need to learn how. You were not born knowing how to drive a car, but somehow at some point in your life you learned how to drive one. The same is true for productivity—maybe you weren't born being a naturally productive person, but you can learn how to be a productive person with just a little bit of study and effort.

8.   **I am not so sure about the term "life balance" anymore**. I tend to think that life balance is a vision, not a mission, and one that is a concept and not a reality. Why do I say that? Because I think people are struggling to achieve life balance, and because of the way life is these days, they are sometimes not able to accomplish it, so they are extremely frustrated about not having life balance. To me this is like trying to find the pot of gold at the end of the rainbow, because you'll never find the end of the rainbow,

or the pot of gold at the end—it is total mythology (sorry to disappoint you). I am sure I will get a few letters from the Leprechauns Union. My view is that life balance is more of an ebb and flow process. What do I mean by that? I think that some weeks it is likely that you can have life balance. However, in the real world there are going to be some weeks where it is literally impossible to have life balance. For example, if I have a packed speaking calendar and I speak five days in five cities, I'm sure that my week is not going to have much balance. There will be some aspects of my life that week that will not get the attention that they deserve because I am in five cities in five days. Let's say, for example, you have a huge project at work that has a looming deadline and that deadline is going to make or break your company or your career. I have a feeling that for perhaps months your life is not going to be as balanced as it will be when the project is done and complete. I have often thought this is also true for a politician who is running for president. They seem to be on the road for years with very little life balance. So to summarize, I think sometimes you have life balance and sometimes you just won't. Try for it, but don't always expect it.

## WHY AM I WRITING ABOUT PRODUCTIVITY?

Why am I qualified to write a book about productivity? I think that is a very legitimate question. As my wife, Rachael, recently said, "You are the perfect person to write a book about productivity because, boy are you productive!" I have my own business as a professional speaker, writer, and executive coach. I travel around the country speaking and consulting, and I also do executive coaching. I have taught thousands of people how to be more productive in the last 28 years. At the same time, I'm also a regular contributing writer for The Huffington Post,

Entrepreneur, Inc., The Good Men Project, Addicted2success, and several other websites four times a month. In addition, I have written 20 books and hundreds of articles. Often when people hear this list of things that I am regularly working on, they ask me, "How do you find the time?" I don't have any more time than you do, my friend. I don't have a magic time machine in my office. I don't think it's a matter of *finding* the time; it's a matter of *managing* the time and *prioritizing* the time and using systems and processes in order to be more productive. I plan to share with you in this book all of my secrets of how you too can be more productive in any area of life that you choose.

The other reason I wanted to write a book about productivity is that my personal mission is to make a positive difference in other people's lives both at work and at home. Both me and my publisher agree that productivity seems to be a huge pain point with many people in the world. So my goal, my mission, my obsession is to help you reduce your pain by helping you to increase your productivity and to live a more joyful life because you *can be* more productive.

I also have something I want you to think about. I don't want you at the latter part of your life to be suffering from something I call "regret-itis." What is that? It is simply a term that I use to describe a condition where people reach a certain age and they are retired. I think there are many of them who are living with regret, bitterness, and really wish that they could live parts of their life over. The reason for this is there are certain things they should have, could have, would have done that they never did. So they are suffering from the disease of regret-itis. I don't want you to be that person; I want you—*now* at your age (whatever that may be)—to start being more productive so you can achieve your dreams.

## WHAT ARE THE BENEFITS OF JUMPSTARTING YOUR PRODUCTIVITY?

I think there are many benefits of being a more productive person:

### Reduce stress

I think that when you are a more productive person, you feel more satisfied and happy because you are getting things done. You are cooking with gas, you are hitting a home run, you are making the bacon, you are the grand prizewinner! In all seriousness, when you feel like you're achieving what you want and need to achieve, you are much less stressed. Because you can get more done in less time, you're less stressed because you can spend the rest of your time doing other things that may be more relaxing or enjoyable.

### More control

When people jumpstart their productivity, they feel like they're more in control of their work life and their personal life. When you have systems and processes in place to make you more productive, you do have more control, and you feel it, and it is a great feeling.

### Make more money

I do believe that in our society people who are the most compensated are those who can be the *most productive*. They get results. It just makes economic sense that if you can get more done, someone is going to pay you more than those who cannot get more stuff done. Just to clarify, I'm not talking about working more hours, but about getting more done in the hours that you work. Tim Ferriss, the author of the book *The 4-Hour Workweek*, actually took this to the ultimate extreme. When he was the owner of a company, he got his work hours down to only four hours per week. He then took his techniques and turned them into a book called *The 4-Hour Workweek*. I have also noticed that most people who are extremely wealthy are not only more productive, but they're more productive because they are more in control of how they manage their time. So if you would like to make more money, becoming more productive can and will help you do exactly that.

### Achieve your dreams

I think that if you're able to get a handle on productivity, you're much closer to being able to achieve your dreams and make them happen. I have met many entrepreneurs who started businesses on the weekends and at night while also holding down a full-time job. Their ability to be incredibly productive at their regular job also allowed them to be productive in building their entrepreneurial dream when they were not working at their regular job. So if you want to achieve your dreams, you have to figure out how to be more productive. As Larry the Cable Guy once said, you can "Git-R Done."

### Be a better parent

Yes, I know you think your eyes may be deceiving you. Did you just read "be a better parent"? Yes, I sincerely and honestly believe that if you are a more productive person, you can also be a better parent. How? Well, if you are able to achieve what you need to get done at work, then you will work fewer hours and be able to be around your family more. I also think that if you are more productive at home and when doing the day-to-day activities required to manage a household, then you will be able to spend more time with your children. Lastly, a side effect of all of this, which many people do not think about, is you can be a good parent by teaching your kids how to be more productive by modeling it for them. This way they end up becoming productive adults themselves. How great a legacy would that be to leave?

## WHAT IS COVERED IN THIS BOOK?

In this book, we're going to cover a lot of information to help jumpstart your productivity and give you ten jolts. So pull out your battery cables and get ready for a charge!

### 1. *Set goals or go home*

In this chapter, we will talk about the critical importance of setting goals in order to be more productive. I'm guessing you will be very shocked that research shows that only about 3% of the population has clearly articulated goals. That means that 97% of the population does not have clearly articulated goals and that they don't really know what it is that they're going after. After all you can't hit a target if you don't know what it is. You can't go on a journey unless you know your final destination. To me, goals are the map that help you get where it is you want to go, and productivity helps you get there. As I often say, it's great to be productive, but what do you want to be productive *about*? So in this chapter, I will guide you through how to define your goals in both your professional and personal life and to write them down so that you know how to apply the productivity to the right areas of your life.

### 2. *Don't fight the system*

One of the terms that  is very popular in today's world is talking about using "hacks" to improve your life in every sort of way you think of. I like to think of time systems as hacks or methodologies to help you get better at managing your time, which helps you to be more productive. In this chapter, I will talk about some of the tools that you can use to manage your time more effectively by using some sort of time management system. Sometimes when I ask people in my productivity programs what type of time management system they use, they give me really funny answers such as 1) a legal pad, 2) sticky notes, 3) a whiteboard (I'm not sure how you carry a wall-size whiteboard into a meeting—just saying), 4) nothing—they use no time management system at all. Ironically, number four was made by a participant whose company invested thousands of dollars every year into buying each associate a time management calendar book. It doesn't matter to me what time management system you use; all that matters is the fact that you use one. That time management system can be either a digital tool (computer, ohone, iPad) or a handwritten tool like a paper calendar. Each type of system has advantages and disadvantages; we will cover what they are, and you can decide which one works best for you. Not every runner needs the same running shoes. Some people like one type, others another. The key is to find the one that works for you.

### 3. Time wasting

In this chapter, I'll share with you some of the shocking statistics from the United States Bureau of Labor and Industry, which I think will fascinate you about the way that people use their time both at work and at home. For example, did you know that the average American spends 2.8 hours watching television per day? Are we as a society really couch potatoes? One of the things that I found in working with lots of folks both in speaking and in coaching is that many people are not aware of how much time they waste on items that are what I would call "fluff." There are time-wasting activities such as the Internet, watching television, and spending time on social media like Twitter and Facebook that end up costing us a lot of time, effort, and energy. They do not really make huge contributions to our life. They are like cotton candy, delicious but not very nutritious. I don't want you to get the wrong impression; I'm not saying that you should never ever watch TV, and I'm not saying you should never be on Facebook and post messages for your friends and family about one thing or another, and they about you. But what I am saying is I would like you to analyze how much time you spend on each of those elements because I think you will be very surprised how much time is occupied in those innocent yet time-sucking activities. I've often said that at the end of your life you will not regret having missed an episode of some TV show. What you will regret is not having done something that was more significant that you wanted to achieve but did not. As Dick Van Dyke once said, "For some reason, as time gets short in life, wasting time escaping through entertainment bothers me."

### 4. *Can I have a compass please?*

Planning your activities is the next important element after you have a solid time management system in place, and you know what your goals and objectives are. To me, the planning of activities is central to being a highly productive person. In this chapter, I would give you some tools and techniques to help you plan your activities, including how to plan better in terms of business and personal travel, how to do a better job planning a project, and how to analyze all your activities to make sure that they are as efficient as possible. The problem is that all of us as human beings fall into the trap of doing a habit and continuing the habit pretty much for the rest of our adult lives. My goal is to get you to analyze all your habits related to planning activities and to look very carefully at the ones you can *change* in order to get dramatically better results. For example, when I go on a business trip I have an interesting technique my wife taught me for planning my travel. The technique is that when I set out I have my GPS. But I also make sure to print out Google maps for every leg of my journey and have them printed and in my possession so I have a backup if the navigation system fails. I used to think this was a technique that was a little over the top until one day my navigation system failed, and guess what? The paper saved me. That's just one of the examples of processes you can put into place to make your travel easier, less stressful, and less laborious.

### 5. Sunrise or sunset

In this chapter, we will take a look at whether you are a morning or an evening person. But you see that's not really the question; the question is not whether you are a morning or an evening person, a night owl or an early bird. What matters is trying to figure out when you are *most productive*. There is no doubt in my mind that there are times of day when you are certainly much more productive than others. In this chapter, I will help you evaluate when you're at your best and what activities you should do when you're at your best as well as when you're at your least level of focus and what to do at those times of the day when you're at your lowest point of energy and effectiveness.

### 6. Doing the do

How do you know what you are going to work on today? When I ask people this question I often get very humorous responses. Sometimes the answer is "I just take the day as it comes," or "I wait to see what it is that I need to work on once I get into the office," or "I find out what my boss wants me to work on." With all due respect, you need to start out with a plan, which is simply a piece of paper (or any device) with something on it called a "to-do list." I think a to-do list is a very powerful tool because *it gives you a track to run on for the day; it helps you know what it is that you have done and what it is you still need to do.* I think now in today's fast-paced high-technology environment a to-do list becomes even more important because it's easy to lose track and focus of what it is we are working on. In this chapter, I'll give you some tips and techniques for making sure that your to-do list works for you in the way that it should.

### 7. Thumbs down

I think one of the other issues about productivity is the idea that we think that we have to do everything for everyone and that we have to be yes-men and yes-women. Is it truly a battle between quantity and quality? In this chapter, I'll talk about how to decline invitations gracefully, and, perhaps more importantly, how to negotiate with people who ask you to do things and want them done ASAP. The problem with many terms we use in business is they are extremely vague. For example ASAP means as soon as possible, but each person's definition of as soon as possible is different. Your definition may be entirely different, and therein lies the rub that creates lots of problems.

### 8. Pardon the interruption

With the current popularity of the open office environment, it seems like no one has an office or even a cubicle; everybody seems to be suffering from constant and continuous interruption. When there are no walls and no cubes, everyone thinks it's okay to approach you at any time of the day to talk to you or to see if you can solve a problem that they are working on. I wonder when that became okay? The problem is that if you do not control the interruptions, the interruptions won't just be an interruption to that part of the day but will interrupt the entire day. So I believe it then becomes your responsibility to control and manage the interruptions as they come up throughout the day.

### 9. I have a robot

In this chapter, I'll talk about how you can effectively use technology to get more done now. I remember as a young child in school watching films that said that technology is going to allow man to be so productive in the future that he would have to work only 20 hours a week. Now, of course, we find that concept humorous, but the reality is technology can make our lives easier and can significantly contribute to us being more productive and effective. You just have to use it as your tool to increase your productivity. In this chapter, I will share with you the technology to help you become much more effective and less frustrated while trying to get everything done.

### 10. The power of rest and relaxation

While most of this book will be aimed at how to be more productive at work, I think it is also important to talk about the power of rest, recovery, and relaxation. If you become more productive, you will have more time for rest and relaxation, but the irony is that even as you become more productive, you still need to schedule time (yes, I said schedule) in order to recharge your batteries, unwind, and relax in order to be as productive as possible when you go back to work.

### 11. Follow the law

In the last chapter of the book, I will share with you what I believe to be the 10 most powerful principles of productivity in order for you to be more productive and effective in everything that you do at work and at home. You only get one life (as far as I know); the idea is to make sure that you live what I refer to as a maximum life.

Are you ready to have fun, and engage in some deep thinking about productivity and get fully engaged to live a life of maximum joy achievement, feeling like you are living life on purpose? Let's go ahead and get started, shall we?

# CHAPTER ONE

## *JOLT #1*
# SET GOALS AND WRITE THEM DOWN

## Target-Based Goal Setting

*"You got to know what you want. This is central to acting on your intentions. When you know what you want, you realize that all there is left then is time management. You manage your time to achieve your goals because you clearly know what you're trying to achieve in your life."*
—Patch Adams

If we're going to talk about productivity, then we have to decide what we are going to be *productive about*. We can't know what we're going to be productive about if we did not decide what it is we are trying to achieve in life. Why should you set goals for yourself personally and professionally?

### *You can't hit a target if you don't know what it is*

There is not an army in the world that would ever go out to battle without knowing exactly what their mission is. There isn't a contractor in the world who would build a house without having a clearly drawn blueprint before they started. There isn't a director in the world who would start filming a movie without first knowing exactly what the vision was in the form of a script before they started. There isn't a symphony conductor in the world that would conduct a symphony without both them and everyone on the team having a score and without rehearsing it first. But yet, surprisingly and very shockingly, there are many people in the world who have never taken the time, the energy, and the effort to decide what it is they're trying to achieve in the form of written goals. They just don't have them, and they have never taken the time to write them down.

### It helps in your planning

When you have goals, it helps you in your daily planning because you now know what it is that you're striving to do so that you can put together an exact plan on how to get there.

### It helps you make better decisions

When you have clarity of goals, then when situations come up it helps you make better decisions. As a professional speaker and book author, and as a columnist for several large websites, I'm often approached by people with various business opportunities. They are always very fascinating and often come by e-mail or by phone or in person. When those opportunities arise, I have to use the goals that we have as an organization to evaluate whether it's a good decision or a bad one. If you don't have goals, how can you know whether a decision is a sound one or not? When you have goals you are also much more comfortable in making decisions because they are based on the foundational principles of the goals you have.

### It is very motivating

When you take the time and energy to write down your goals, it is extremely motivating to think about your future potential, short term, mid term, and long term. As Robert Schuller once said, "Goals are not only absolutely necessary to motivate us. They are essential to really keep us alive. I do believe that people who don't have goals become stagnant and not nearly as motivated as people who do have them."

### It increases your credibility

When you have clearly articulated goals and you know what they are, it increases your credibility with all the people who work around you. When people ask why you want to do something and how, you are going to be able to answer that question, having goals in the background. The fact that you can talk about the goals enhances your credibility because you're a person who is thoughtful and prepared. Translation—you're someone who has their act together. People at work want to work with somebody who has their act together as opposed to somebody who doesn't. As I travel around the country as a speaker and trainer, the biggest complaint that I hear is leaders who don't really have an idea where they are going and have no clearly articulated goals for their organizations.

### Setting goals helps improve your thinking

I really feel like there are way too many people in life who are, as I describe it, flying by the seat of their pants. One of the reasons is they have not taken the time to think through and articulate their goals professionally and personally. The act of setting goals is not just the activity of setting them but also the process of thinking through and then deciding what it is that you want and what it is that you don't want. It's not merely the activity of setting a goal; it's the activity of thinking more deeply. It is thinking about the short-term, mid-term, and long-term goals. As an executive coach, I work very often with clients who have no clearly articulated goals. With our executive coaching process we are able to help them come up with clearly articulated goals for their life. The only reason they're able to do this is that I force them to think through what it is that they truly want for their life personally and professionally. We are helping them define a target.

### It helps you with how you spend your time

Let's imagine that time is a bank account and that every hour that you spend at work is a withdrawal from that account. We all have the same amount, and we all have the same number of hours available. When you have clearly articulated goals, it helps you determine how you want to invest and spend your time or where you don't want to invest the time. Once you have clearly articulated goals, you will know where you are wasting your time and where you want to spend more time in order to be more productive as it relates to the goals.

## THE FIRST STEP IN DEFINING YOUR GOALS

Okay cowboys and cowgirls, here is the first step in defining your goals, and pay careful attention if you are going on the trail called life: you must define them. We need to put on our goal hats. So the question that I was getting from people that attend my programs is, "*how* do I define my goals?" Here is a thought: in my mind, the question is not really how to define your goals, but what it is that you want.

I was once coaching a vice president of a large corporation. When I asked her what her goal was, she said that her goal was to become a senior vice president. When I asked her why, she said her reason was that it was the next box on the organizational chart. I said, "Really? I understand it is easy to look at that next box on the organizational chart as your goal, but you are, in my opinion, jumping the gun—my real question is *why* do you want to be a senior vice president?" She then picked up the sheet with the organizational chart on it and circled the boxes and said, "Because that's where I want to go." I paused for a moment and said to her, "You're telling me that you want to move a chess piece from one box to another, but you can't really tell me why; you can only tell me that you want the piece to be moved. So here is why I bring up the story: I really think you need to go through the exercise of defining *what it is that you want* in order to define your goals.

I want you to set aside some time, find somewhere where you can concentrate, and take out a piece of paper or your laptop and just think about what you want.

### Step One:

I want you to look at each category of your life. (These are just some suggestions; you can modify or make your own categories):

- Professional

- Social

- Love

- Financial

- Mental/intellectual

- Physical and health

- Family

- Friends

- Hobbies and recreation

- Spiritual

- Civic/community

### Step Two:

On your paper or laptop, write out each category, leaving plenty of room under each category to write out what it is that you want in each area. I just want you to think through each category and decide what it is you truly want for each area. Here are some questions that you might use to guide yourself in each particular category:

1. As it relates to this category—what am I passionate about?

2. As it relates to this category—what is it that I truly want?

3. As it relates to this category—what will truly make me happy?

4. As it relates to this category—what will make me feel the most fulfilled?

5. As it relates to this category—what would be the ultimate position?

6. As it relates to this category—what do I dream of doing?

7. As it relates to this category—what do I dream of being?

8. As it relates to this category—how would I know it when I was successful?

9. As it relates to this category—why do I want it?

10. As it relates to this category—what will be my reward if I am successful?

11. If I had all the money in the world—what would I want to do?

So let me give you an example. Let's say in the category of "professional," someone writes down:

"I am truly passionate about being in a creative industry. I love creating things."

On question two, they say, "What I really want to do is to create great advertisements or advertising campaigns that will help me fulfill my need to create new ideas and concepts."

In answer to question three, they say, "What would truly make me happy is working in a creative services department of the company or for a progressive and highly creative advertising agency, doing the work that I love."

In answer to question four, they would say, "What makes me feel fulfilled is having my work rewarded and appreciated, and being able to make a contribution."

In answer to question five, they may say, "I think my ultimate position would either be an art director, a creative director, or owning my own advertising or creative services agency."

In answer to question six, they may say, "I dream of doing work where I'm free to express my creativity as many ways as possible in a fun, creative environment."

In answer to question seven, they may say, "I don't think the answer to question seven is much different than the answer to question six, except a dream of being successful."

In answer to question eight, they may say, "I would know I am successful when I was promoted, my work was appreciated, and I was given full autonomy to do my work with as little oversight as possible."

In answer to question nine, they may say, "Because I believe that this is the work that I was born to do, work that I'm the most passionate about. I just have to find the right place to do it."

In answer to question ten, they may say, "Fulfillment and financial rewards."

The next step, of course, would be to write your answers down in each category. One quick note: categories that I provided are just suggestions; you can come up with your own categories. You may also want to do this exercise over several weeks in several sessions, because each time you sit down to look at your answers and think through them, they may be somewhat different and you can compare them.

This will really give you a very good idea about what it is that you actually want, and you may even want to have discussions with friends and family, and ask them what they think about your ideas and see if they have any additional input. Some people may have ideas you had not thought about.

Here are some ideas to think about related to each category:

### Professional

When you think about your profession, I want to caution you to guard against wanting a certain position. If you're talking about what it is that you want, I suggest that you think about the kind of work you want to be doing, not about a specific title.

I think it is a little silly to say, "I want to be senior vice president of engineering," instead of saying, "This is the kind of work that I want to be doing and this is what I want for my career." Why do I say that? Because if you decide what kind of work you want to do, then you can evaluate whether the position that you aspire to fills those wants and needs or not. Far too often people aspire to a position because it appeals to their ego or to the prestige of the title, but end up being miserable because it's not really what they want to do. So keep this question in mind: as you go through every one of these categories, you need to ask yourself *what do I want?*

### Social

When you think about your social life and what you want to get from your social life, I think what you have to determine is what you find most enjoyable. Some people like being part of large groups, socializing with many people. How active do you want your social life to be? Some people like socializing in small groups and socializing with only a few people. I want you to think about what makes you happiest and most fulfilled socially. How do you determine what fulfillment looks like? I think one of the ways to make that determination is if you go to a social event (let's say dinner with friends), later you can analyze how you feel about the evening. To me the best litmus tests are 1) Do you feel happy? 2) Do you feel energized? 3) Do you feel liked, maybe even loved? 4) Do your social activities make you a better person in terms of the way you feel? To me those are good ways of looking at your social activities and whether they work for you or not.

### Love

When I say love, I'm talking about being in a relationship with someone who loves you and whom you love in return. Several years ago, I was on a hike with a group of people and was talking to a woman who was walking along beside me during the hike. She told me that she was a widower and her husband died several years ago. After much discussion I asked if she thought about being married again in the future. She said with a rather bitter tone that she was "done with men" and really wanted to be alone. That is okay if that is what you want. Don't get me wrong— I'm not saying there may be phases in your life you prefer to be alone, but I do believe it is the human condition not to want to be alone and to want to be loved. So when you ask yourself the questions about love, I think it is very important to determine what it is that you want out of a loving relationship. Do you have criteria in regard to whom you are looking for? If you are already in a loving relationship, then what do you want your relationship to be like? I have been married to my wife for almost 3 years, and we decided from a very early part of our relationship that when we got married, we would work toward an *extraordinary marriage*, because that's what both of us wanted, and that's what both of us have.

### Financial

I think it is very important to determine what you want financially. When I talk to our financial planner he tells me that one of the biggest mistakes to make financially is not to thinkabout finances and money earlier in life. So think about what you want in terms of how much money you make in the short term, mid term, and long term but also perhaps, most importantly, what you want to do with the money that you make. Some people accumulate a lot of money to buy the houses and the cars and the toys, and some people who have a lot of money live modestly and give to charity or help out the world. I'm not saying that either one is the *right choice*, but I'm urging you to think about what you want in terms of finances.

## Mental/intellectual

In many of my programs that I teach, I talk about the idea that when most people graduate from school they attend a commencement ceremony. Once they graduate, people often tell themselves they are done learning and reading, school is over! The reality is *commencement* means "to begin." The other reality is in order to be successful in life I believe that you have to be continuously learning, growing, and developing new skills. It is not a good idea to become stagnant. I offer a proprietary leadership program called *Lessons in Leadership,* which is a six-day program. It consists of one full class day each month for six months. During the program I assign three books to each program participant to read. In a program that I was teaching several months ago, one of the folks in the class came over and said on a break: "Gee, Shawn, I really appreciate you *making us* read this book; I have not read a book since college. In fact, I was sitting in our living room the other night reading a book, and my wife came in from the kitchen and was extremely shocked to see me reading!" In the category of mental and intellectual, I just want you to decide what it is that you want to know, what it is that you want to learn, what it is that you need to learn that would help keep you stimulated and motivated mentally and intellectually. As a side note, I think if you are reading, it is perfectly okay to read fiction, but I recommend broadening your intellectual horizons by also reading more nonfiction.

## Physical and health

How is your health? What I mean by that is, how is your health in terms of lifestyle habits, dietary habits, and your level of physical fitness? This is entirely up to you to make life choices about your health and wellness, but here is something I want you to think about. I don't believe that you can be the most effective you if you're not in good physical health and enjoying a good level of wellness. People who are in shape and are healthy are *more productive* and get more done because they have more energy. I also believe that people that are in good shape and healthy feel better about themselves in terms of their self-esteem, which also leads to their being more productive. Why is that? I think they're willing to try more things because they have the confidence to try them. So in this category I want you to ask yourself, what would be the ultimate version of you in terms of this category? If you made a change, which one would help you the most in this category? I can't make any decisions for you in any of these categories, but I urge you to think about them deeply, because your answers in each one of these categories will lead to your being more productive.

### Family

If you have a family, what do you want your family to be like in terms of your home family environment? If you don't have a family at home, then you are certainly part of an immediate family, meaning your parents and your siblings. Do you want to have a family in the future? If so, what do you see that family looking like? So what do you want your family to be like? If you have children, what kind of family do you want your children to grow up in? What do you want your family to be like when you go home at the end of the day for you and for them?

### Hobbies and recreation

I think a great question to ask yourself about hobbies and recreation is:

- What are you passionate about?

- What do you love doing?

- What are those activities that you do that make it seem as if time is flying by?

I love doing lots of things, and it may not come as a great surprise, but one thing I love doing is reading nonfiction books. When I am immersed in a great book I can read for two hours and it will seem as if it was only two minutes that I'd been absorbed in that book.

In the hobbies and recreation category, I would recommend thinking about what you want to continue doing in terms of hobbies and recreation, but I would also investigate some of the hobbies and recreational activities you may want to start doing or that you would like to do.

### Spiritual
It is completely up to you to decide what this means to you.

## THE SECOND STEP IN DEFINING YOUR GOALS

I know you are reading a book about productivity, and for some people it may seem puzzling to have just developed a list of all the things that you want. But trust me, there is a method to my madness. Now that you have developed a list of your wants in each life category, you're ready to write down your goals for each of these categories on the basis of the ones that you have identified.

To give you a big picture, here is how all the pieces fit together:

**Wants ➔ Written Goals ➔ Plans ➔ Productivity**

So now you can see how all the elements fit together. I recommend carefully reviewing each list of things that you want and the answers to all the questions that you reviewed. Then write down one or two goals for each of the categories. Here are a few tips about writing down your goals:

### Specific

Make sure that you write down goals that are as specific as possible. For example, in the financial category don't just write down a goal of "make more money." Instead, write down a goal of increasing your compensation by 20% by the end of the year. As Napoleon Hill once said, *"a goal is a dream with a deadline."*

### In writing

You'll notice that I emphasized that the goals should be in writing, not just in verbal form. All the research indicates the goals are much more effective if they are written instead of being verbal. There are several reasons for this, but the short explanation of writing down your goals is that it makes you much more effective because you are holding yourself accountable and you are activating something in your brain called a reticular activating system.

Almost every successful person I know has written goals, and they are posted where they can be reviewed on a frequent and consistent basis. This morning when I first sat down at my desk, I did not turn on my computer and start checking e-mail. Instead, I reviewed my written goals to remind myself of what I'm working on and reviewed my list of things that I need to do today relating to those goals.

### It's very motivating

If you write down your goals as they relate to health and fitness, and if you determine you want to be a certain weight or a certain body percentage by the end of the year, giving you a goal to work on, it is extremely motivating to think about the end result.

## THE LAST STEP IN DEFINING YOUR GOALS

So once your goals are identified and they are cemented into each of their respective categories and they are in writing, you are ready to take the next step, which is a big one and also essential to ensuring that you are productive. As Brian Tracy once said, "people with clear, written goals accomplish far more in a shorter period of time than people without them could ever imagine."

The goals now become the compass to help point you toward what it is you want to be productive about. You can't work and be more productive if you do not know what it is you're working toward.

The next step after you have your list of goals would be to think about the increments of time. The time increments of your goals will be as follows:

- Yearly

- Quarterly

- Monthly

- Weekly

- Daily

The idea would then be to take your list of goals and transfer them over to your calendaring system (may be a physical calendar or an electronic calendar), and once you have written them down in your calendar system, you can then arrange the goals in those respective time elements.

Next you have to take your goals, and after writing them out ask yourself specifically what individual actions you need to do to make sure that your goals are achieved.

There would be your list of goals and in addition to it all the activities that are aligned with each one.

Let's take a look at an example:

### Yearly

Let's say in your yearly goals you write down a goal as follows: "My goal is to be the salesperson of the year for my organization nationally by increasing my sales 45% in the coming year. That means in the coming year I need to have $5 million in sales."

### Quarterly

Once you have nailed down the annual goal of becoming the salesperson of the year for your organization nationally, you know how much you need to increase the sales and the number that you are looking for.

The next question you have to ask yourself is how to go about doing that? So the reality is you need to take that number and divide it into a quarter of the year, which would mean for quarter one you would need to have $1.5 million in sales.

Now that you know that the quarterly goal is to do $1.5 million, you need to figure out what activities need to be done in order to accomplish that.

The activities you may use in order to achieve the goals are as follows:

- Read one book on sales effectiveness in quarter one

- Attend a one-day training program in quarter one

- Analyze all my accounts and figure out how to increase incremental revenue

- Increase account penetration by 15%

- Close three new accounts in quarter one

- Review all sales files to see if I can reactivate some old clients

- Offer existing clients new goods and services

## Monthly

Once the hard work has been done for the annual goals and for the quarterly goals, it's relatively easy to then take those activities that you've decided are essential for success in quarter one and transfer them over to the monthly calendar to determine what is needed in month one in order to get off on the right foot to achieve the goals in quarter one. So of the six options that you came up with for quarterly activities, pick one and make sure that you achieve it in month one.

## Weekly

Once you have your monthly activities and goals in place and know exactly what you need to do that month, take all the activities for the month and divide them into week one, two, three, and four and record them in your time management system. Maybe think of this as a funnel system where we put our annual goals in the very top of the funnel; it is very wide, but as we work through each step in the process from yearly to quarterly to monthly to weekly, the funnel gets narrower and you funnel it down all the way to your weekly and daily activities.

## Daily

It stands to reason that once I have established some activities for the week, I know exactly what I need done Monday through Friday. I would then take those activities and divide them over the five days in my time management system. This would all end up going to your daily task list, which we will discuss in more detail in a later chapter.

If you do the work of planning what you want, planning your goals, putting them in writing, and then transferring them over to activities that you need to do in order to accomplish those goals, you will be performing a task I call prioritizing and calendarizing. Don't skip this step!

Everyone in the world knows that the only way that something truly gets done is if you:

- Focus on it intensely

- Create a plan

- Put action items on the list

- Put it on your calendar

It will ensure that things get done, and you will be much more productive. As Paul J. Meyer once said, "Productivity is never an accident. It is always the result of a commitment to excellence, intelligent planning, and focused effort."

# WORK IT!

Do you have clearly articulated goals?

_____

_____

_____

_____

Are they in writing? If not, why not?

_____

_____

_____

_____

What has prevented you from having goals in the past?

_____

_____

_____

_____

What are your professional goals in the next 12 months?

_____

_____

_____

_____

What are your personal goals in the next 12 months?

_____

_____

_____

_____

What will be the results if you achieve them?

_____

_____

_____

_____

What resources do you have to help you achieve your goals?

_____

_____

_____

_____

CHAPTER TWO

## JOLT #2
# SELECT AND USE A QUALITY TIME MANAGEMENT SYSTEM

## DON'T FIGHT THE SYSTEM: SELECTING AND USING A TIME MANAGEMENT SYSTEM

*"The secret to modern life is finding the measure in time management. I have two kids, career and I travel, and I don't think my life is any different than most couples. The most valuable commodity now for many people is time and how to parcel that out."*
—HUGH JACKMAN

A pilot would never fly without a flight plan. A contractor would never build a building without a blueprint. A marathon runner would never run a race without a watch to track their pace. Yet many people I have met try to operate their work and life without some kind of time management system. I don't honestly know how they do it.

I once knew a person who did not actually use *any* kind of time management system, and when I asked them they admitted that they did not have one. It's probably no great surprise to you that because they did not have one, they often missed deadlines, missed appointments, and showed up late for conference calls. When other people asked them how this happened they simply stated that "they forgot." If you want to be productive, successful, and credible, one of the main tools that you need is some kind of system in place for managing and tracking your time.

## TYPES OF TIME MANAGEMENT SYSTEMS

There are many kinds of time management systems on the market:

### Phone based

Most phones come with some sort of calendaring time management system.

### Time management system apps

There are a ton of time management apps available that can be used on any device.

### Electronic or online

There are several systems that are desktop- or laptop-based that are tied to an e-mail application (Outlook, for example).

### Hard copy/written

There are many paper-based systems; they are on paper in some form (binder, journal, or book).

### Collaborative

There are some systems that I describe as collaborative time management systems. Some people even call them project management collaboration systems, but I would argue that the big function of those systems is the management of time tracking and scheduling and arranging appointments.

## UPSIDES AND DOWNSIDES OF EACH TYPE OF SYSTEM

Here are some upsides and downsides of each kind of system. I am giving you one or two examples in each category—just so you know they are not endorsements but only examples to provide clarity.

### Phone based

The phone-based type of time management system is very cutting edge and very modern, and certainly is a lightweight way of carrying around a time management system. The downside is I have found that it is more difficult to schedule items in it than in some other time management systems. Plus, as with any other technology you often are relying on the fact that you have a charge, are not running out of power, and your phone that day is actually behaving itself (there some cell phones that just don't behave as they are supposed to). An additional challenge is that you may not be able to access the calendar if the phone does not have a signal. If the system on your phone is also linked to your other time management system (which may be on your desktop or your laptop), then you have the issue of making sure that they "sync" with each other so that updating one updates the other as well. I personally found the whole syncing issue to be a problem when you try to have systems that talk to one another. Sometimes instead of talking to one another, they just argue back and forth!

If you think it is ugly when people argue back and forth, you should see what happens when software argues back and forth; believe me, it is not a pretty sight!

### Time management system apps

There are a ton of time management system apps available that are either free or for purchase. Examples of these would be TimeTune and Todoist. They also come in many different forms: apps for time management, apps for a to-do list, apps for time tracking, and also what I call "hybrid models," for they are a combination of all components. These can be very effective and can be used on the device of your choosing, whether it is your phone, iPad, Kindle, or some other device. The downside is each app has a learning curve, and, of course, you can't use the app unless you actually have a signal on the device that you're using. There is also always the proverbial power issue.

### Electronic or online

There are some distinct upsides to using an online calendar that is based somewhere in the cloud. (I haven't figured out yet where the cloud is located.) Examples of these would be Google Calendar or Outlook. They are often free, and the other advantage is you often have the ability to share your calendar with several others so that they can check your availability in order to set up a meeting. The upside is also a downside, because people can schedule a meeting with you or for you without your permission. Of course, the other distinct disadvantages of an electronic or online time management system are that you are relying on being able to have a signal from whatever device you're using and that you do have to log on to the Internet and use some sort of browser to get to the time management system.

### Hardcopy/written

One of the upsides of having a hard copy time management system is they never need to be updated or charged, and there's no software involved. Examples of these would be Planner Pads or Day Runners. As long as you have it physically available, you can use it as you please. Another upside of having hard copy, paper-based calendars is the fact that you can save them so you can refer back to them over several years. This is an advantage over the electronic or online version that can be limited on how far back you can look in terms of prior time appointments from years past. The downside to paper calendars is they may be perceived as being a little old-fashioned by some, and if you ever lose your paper time management system it's very hard to reconstruct the appointments that you had in writing.

### Collaborative

I think the collaborative time management systems can certainly have advantages, particularly if you work continually with a very close-knit group that has to function on a daily level, working on projects. Examples of these would be Basecamp or Box. The upside is that you can share documents, share information, and send messages. It's particularly helpful if you have a virtual team that is geographically dispersed across a large area of the world. It can also definitely help productivity because you don't have to bother with attaching a file and sending it by e-mail, because the people in the system will automatically be notified that a new file is available and they can get the file and work on it. The downside of collaborative systems is that they do not work very well for an individual tracking time, only for time tracking in the group.

## DECIDING WHAT KIND OF TIME MANAGEMENT SYSTEM TO USE

I think what is very important is to think about what kind of time management system you want to use. A quick search of time management systems on Google indicates that there are literally *thousands* of time management systems available online for purchase. If you do a quick search on your phone for time management apps, you will find that there are literally thousands of apps available to help manage your time and your productivity. I think the key is to try to discover what time management system works best for you. So how do you go about making that determination?

### Ask yourself what it is that you need

When you think about a time management system, what are some of the functions that you want the time management system to help you do? You want to keep track of appointments? You want to keep track of projects? You want to keep track of contacts, phone numbers, and addresses? Keep a list of things to do? Well, you get the idea; I really do believe before you search for the appropriate time management system you should come up with a criteria list of what you're really looking for so you know when you have found it.

### Features to consider

When you are looking at and are reviewing a time management system, here are some elements that you may want to look at to help your evaluation:

#### What is the cost of the time management system?

Is it a one-time cost or a recurring monthly fee?

### How easy is it for you to use?

The system you use may be effective, but how easy is it to use on a daily basis? Is there a great deal of training required in order to understand how to use it?

### Is it user friendly for you?

Anytime you use an app, even though it may work well for many other people, the big question to ask is, does it work well for you?

### Is it quick?

Can you do something quickly?

### Does it integrate with the rest of your technology?

I'm certainly not an IT professional, but one thing I think is important to think about is integration. Is the time management system you use compatible, and can it be integrated, with the other technology that you already have? Let's say, for example, you selected a time management app that is really great for your phone. The question is this—does the time management system on your phone synchronize with the time management system on your laptop or your desktop (if that is what you're trying to achieve). For example, if you work for a company and everyone in the company schedules their appointments with some sort of calendar system, it will not help you if the time management system you selected for your phone does not synchronize with the company calendaring system. If you have a time management system that is on paper, can you then transfer your paper appointments over to the electronic version and avoid making errors on each? So those are things to think about in terms of integration and matching systems so that you avoid spending a lot of time going back and forth between both. That would definitely be counterproductive.

### Do you like using it?

Even though this is not an objective criterion, I think this subject is very important. If you do not like using the time management system that you selected, you're going to be reluctant to use it on a regular and consistent basis. Every time you use the time management system you're going to be irritated and will not be very happy about what it is you're using.

### Ask other people

If you were to ask me what kind of time management system I use, I would tell you the brand of time management system that I use. If you were to ask my wife Rachael (who is the author of *Organize Your Business*), she would tell you the time management systems she uses. Keep in mind that no matter whom you ask, they will give you their opinion of what *works for them* and only for them. It would not necessarily work for you. The idea of asking other people is to find out some of the systems that are available and how people like them so you can then review them to determine whether they're going to work for you or not. It is up to you to decide which one works best for you and which one will make you more productive and more comfortable in managing your time and activities. When it comes to time management systems, I do not believe that one size fits all. For example, some people like the time management system that has a weekly or a monthly view, and some people prefer systems that literally just show a daily view. Again, there are no right or wrong answers.

### Don't just settle for a system

I can tell you on a personal level that I spent several years experimenting with different kinds of time management systems. I do not want to endorse a particular product. It doesn't matter what kind I use; what matters is that I spent the time and effort to research which one works best for me. Take the time to do research to find out what systems are out there based on the categories I mentioned earlier. One great thing about application-based time management systems is you can subscribe to them and then cancel them at any time. You get a chance to "test drive" them to see if they will work for you or not. Try a lot of different approaches and find one that really works for you. Then stick to it.

### Develop a list of criteria

One way of determining what kind of system you want is to make a list of specific criteria that you want in your time management system. What is a criteria list? It just literally is a list of what you're looking for in a time management system in terms of those items you would find acceptable and those you would find unacceptable.

There is no right or wrong answer as to what type you should use. The best kind of system for you is one that works. A solid system should make you more organized, more productive, and less stressed. Once you have selected the system that seems to work for you, here are some guidelines that you may find helpful.

## SOME GUIDELINES ABOUT TIME MANAGEMENT SYSTEMS

### Use it

Believe it or not, the system works for you only if you use it consistently. It's analogous to following a dietary/nutrition plan. If you do not follow the plan, you won't get the results that you want. As strange as it sounds, I do know people who have purchased time management systems, and sometimes they use them and sometimes they don't. This is an invitation to be very unproductive.

### Use it for work and home

I have met many people who told me that they have *two* time management systems. One system is for work and the other is for home. I know that people have good reasons for keeping a separate personal system (privacy, for example, may be one), but, generally speaking, I think it is a terrible idea to have two separate time management systems because they don't relate to one another, and this is an invitation for having overlapping appointments and wasting time. What if your kid's important championship game is scheduled at the same time as an important business trip you need to make? If you have more than one time management system, then you may not know that there is a conflict. I recommend having one time management system for all things and posting everything that you have to do there.

### Make sure to record all appointments in your system

One key concept about being more productive is not to have to *remember* anything. Don't rely on or overwhelm your poor overworked brain. It already has too much to remember. When you record all of your appointments in your time management system, the system will remind you when you have an appointment either electronically or on paper. If you try to keep track of appointments in your head, you just have too much data to store and you will invariably end up forgetting an appointment. Each time you make an appointment, record it into your time management system right away. Then it is off your mental plate.

## *Make sure to include details about appointments*

If you make an appointment with a new dentist, for example, in your system don't just write down "appointment with dentist." Be sure to write down the dentist's name, e-mail address, phone number, address of the dental practice, and the dentist's first and last name. This will certainly help make you more productive for a few reasons: 1) if you wait until the day of your appointment to look up the address, you'll be scrambling around trying to find the address that you will be traveling to, and 2) navigation systems work only when you have an address to put into the system. Some people argue that putting in all of the data around the appointment is a very time-consuming task. I really believe it only takes you a few extra minutes to write down the rest of the information about your appointment, instead of scrambling around for the information at the last minute on the day of the appointment. I also recommend if you're meeting with someone, exchange cell phone numbers with them. That way, if you are traveling or have a conflict or are going to be late, you can call them and let them know where you are.

## *Record your goals and your action items*

As I mentioned in the last chapter, once you have your goals and your action items identified, you should then transfer them over into your time management system, listing the activities that you're going to do for the year, for the quarter, and for the month, then weekly and daily. This way you will always have your goals to refer to within the system itself.

## *Have your time management system with you*

I have seen several instances where people are having a meeting, and then when dates are being discussed, they say, "Let me check out that date and get back to you." If they had their time management system with them (a paper version) or if they had an electronic device that can be used to access their system (a phone or iPad), then they would be able to look and see if they were available for that date. This increases your productivity because it increases your efficiency, you decide on a date *right then,* which is one step, instead of having to take two steps in order to complete the transaction. One of the big keys of productivity is to try to eliminate steps in your process, so anytime you can go from two steps to one you save time, effort, and energy. Always focus on reducing anything to as few steps as possible. Let me give you a real-life example. As a professional speaker I travel often. As part of my travel plans, I use a specific website for booking all my hotel reservations. Once I have done all of the research, and I have decided which hotel to reserve and I have booked it, I could then close out the website because the reservation is confirmed. But if you think about it, I missed a few steps. What I should do while I'm already there is 1) go ahead and forward the hotel reservation to my wife and 2) print out the reservation for my travel trip folder. The idea is that when I'm ready for my trip, I do not have to log back on to the same reservation site and do the other two steps. It is much more productive for me to do those steps because I am already there.

### Review your system at the beginning of the week

If you work Monday through Friday, I strongly recommend that you take time late Sunday night to lay out your plan *for the week* in your time management system, and review all appointments that you have that week. You also need to determine what specific meetings you have to prepare for and put the meeting preparation into your time management system. As a quick note, it's important to record and account for all activities in your time management system. Far too often, people do not put one hour of planning for a certain meeting into the time management system, and they are pressed for time because it was not accounted for in the system itself. So by reviewing your time commitments at the very beginning of the week, you start your week off on the right foot and you hit the ground running on Monday morning in order to be successful.

# CHAPTER THREE

## JOLT #3
# BE AWARE OF HOW YOU ARE WASTING YOUR EFFORTS AND ENERGY

## PRODUCTIVITY VAMPIRES: ACTIVITIES THAT SUCK AWAY YOUR PRODUCTIVITY

*"Cell phones, mobile e-mail, and all the other cool and slick gadgets can cause massive losses in our creative output and overall productivity."*
—ROBIN SHARMA

There is an evil force that is unleashed in the world; it is a force that is sometimes invisible and sometimes visible, but it's what I call "productivity vampires." Productivity vampires are the forces that prevent you from being able to accomplish what you want to accomplish and that interfere with your level of productivity. I think one of the biggest challenges that most people face is they are not consciously aware of what the productivity vampires are and how they affect us in such a dramatic way. My goal in this book is to get you to be consciously aware of every activity and consciously aware of the activities that drain your productivity and interfere with your being able to achieve your dreams and hopes and goals. I want you to live a life consciously and on purpose, and part of that is being aware of how you spend every minute of your day in terms of time management and how you focus your activities that are aligned with your short-, mid-, and long-term goals.

Here are some stunning statistics from the US Bureau of Labor about how Americans spend their time. I think you'll find these stats quite shocking, but this is certainly evidence that productivity vampires are lurking around every corner.

## WORKING (BY EMPLOYED PERSONS) IN 2015

- Employed persons worked an average of 7.6 hours on the days they worked. More hours were worked, on average, on weekdays than on weekends—8.0 hours compared with 5.6 hours.

- On the days they worked, employed men worked 42 minutes more than employed women. This difference partly reflects women's greater likelihood of working part time. However, even among full-time workers (those usually working 35 hours or more per week), men worked longer than women—8.2 hours compared with 7.8 hours.

- On the days they worked, 82 percent of employed persons did some or all of their work at their workplace, and 24 percent did some or all of their work at home. Employed persons spent more time working at the workplace than at home—8.0 hours compared with 3.2 hours.

- The share of workers doing some or all of their work at home grew from 19 percent in 2003—the first year the American Time Use Survey (ATUS) was conducted—to 24 percent in 2015. In this same period, the average time employed persons spent working at home on days they worked increased by 40 minutes (from 2.6 hours to 3.2 hours).

- On the days they worked, 38 percent of persons employed in management, business, and financial operations and 35 percent of those employed in professional and related occupations did some or all of their work from home. Workers employed in other occupations were less likely to work from home on days they worked.

- Multiple jobholders were more likely to work on an average day than were single jobholders—80 percent compared with 67 percent. Multiple jobholders were also more likely to work at home than were single jobholders—36 percent compared with 23 percent.

## HOUSEHOLD ACTIVITIES IN 2015

- On an average day, 85 percent of women and 67 percent of men spent some time doing household activities such as housework, cooking, lawn care, or financial and other household management.

- On the days they did household activities, women spent an average of 2.6 hours on such activities, while men spent 2.1 hours.

- On an average day, 22 percent of men did housework—such as cleaning or laundry—compared with 50 percent of women. Forty-three percent of men did food preparation or cleanup, compared with 70 percent of women. Men were slightly more likely to engage in lawn and garden care than were women—12 percent compared with 8 percent.

- From 2003 to 2015, the share of men doing food preparation and cleanup on an average day increased from 35 percent to 43 percent. The average time per day men spent doing food preparation and cleanup increased by 5 minutes, from 16 minutes in 2003 to 21 minutes in 2015.

- From 2003 to 2015, the share of women doing housework on an average day decreased from 54 percent to 50 percent. The average time per day women spent doing housework declined from 58 minutes in 2003 to 52 minutes in 2015.

## LEISURE ACTIVITIES IN 2015

- On an average day, nearly everyone age 15 and over (96 percent) engaged in some sort of leisure activity such as watching TV, socializing, or exercising. Of those who engaged in leisure activities, men spent more time in these activities (5.8 hours) than did women (5.1 hours).

- Watching TV was the leisure activity that occupied the most time (2.8 hours per day), accounting for more than half of leisure time, on average, for those age 15 and over. Socializing, such as visiting with friends or attending or hosting social events, was the next most common leisure activity, accounting for 41 minutes per day.

- Men were more likely than women to participate in sports, exercise, or recreation on a given day—23 percent compared with 18 percent. On days they participated, men also spent more time in these activities than did women—1.7 hours compared with 1.2 hours.

- Time spent reading for personal interest and playing games or using a computer for leisure varied greatly by age. Individuals age 75 and over averaged 1.1 hours of reading per weekend day and 20 minutes playing games or using a computer for leisure. Conversely, individuals ages 15 to 19 read for an average of 8 minutes per weekend day and spent 1.3 hours playing games or using a computer for leisure.

What can we learn from this study? It tells me that people *could be much more productive* than they are. The average American is spending over 5 hours of leisure time per day! This is, by the way, a result of just falling into habits and not thinking about *what we are doing* and *how we are doing it.*

## ANALYZING YOUR PRODUCTIVITY

I believe one of the first aspects of becoming more productive is to analyze exactly how you spend your time every single day, and also what activities you invest your efforts into. So the first step is literally to think through *how you spend your time and efforts* on a weekly basis.

When you work for yourself or for a company, there are activities that you get involved with each week; you need to analyze what those are and whether they are serving your greater purpose. As part of that list here are some things that you need to look at:

### *E-mail*

How much time do you believe that you're spending each week reading and responding to e-mails?

### *Administrative work*

How much time do you believe you're spending each week doing administrative work such as filling out reports, paperwork, expense reports, and any other reporting that's a required responsibility of your job or your profession? Some people jokingly call administrative work "administrivia," but yet we do realize that much of the administrative work we do is entirely necessary in order to successfully run a business, but some of it may not be.

### *Meetings*

How much time and effort do you believe you spend each week attending or participating in live meetings? When I was a vice president in corporate America, I remember very clearly attending meetings most of the day, usually from eight o'clock in the morning until five or six o'clock at night. I often would find that I literally would go from one meeting to another, including a meeting at lunch, which was not just to eat but also to meet with someone about a certain topic.

### Instant messaging

Many organizations now have technology that allows them to instant message other people who work within the company. How much time or effort do you spend each week in some form of instant messaging or texting, which is certainly becoming more prevalent and popular in the world of business?

### Phone calls

How much time and effort do you really believe you spend each week on phone calls with customers, vendors, partners, suppliers, and friends and family?

### Project work

No matter what your profession is, I'm sure you spend a certain amount of time, effort, and energy on projects that you're working on that are short-term, mid-term, or long-term projects.

### Travel

You may be involved in a profession that requires you to travel some of the time. The question is, how much time each week do you spend traveling in order to conduct your business?

### Preparation

All the activities that I listed above require a certain level of preparation in order to participate in those activities. For example, if I'm sending a detailed e-mail, I might have to do some preparation in order to send that e-mail. If I am attending a meeting, I may have to spend 20 minutes (or longer) preparing for that meeting because I may have to discuss data or information.

### Social media

As part of your work as a business professional, how much time are you spending on social media in order to communicate, market, or sell as part of your work? As a note, I'm not talking about the time you spend on social media being social. I mean the time you spend on social media as part of your work.

### Managing/leading

If you're in a managerial or supervisory role, how much time and effort are you spending each week in order to manage and lead the people who report to you directly?

Those are just some of the categories you may be spending your time, effort, and energy on in a typical week. I strongly suggest making a list of all those activities and trying to analyze how much time and effort you spend on average with each of those categories on a weekly basis.

The idea behind this exercise is to really consciously evaluate where you are spending your time and effort to determine 1) whether that's where you should be spending them based on your goals and objectives and 2) where you can become more productive and effective by changing your approach in each of those categories, which will lead to increased productivity.

## PRODUCTIVITY VAMPIRES AND WHAT TO DO ABOUT THEM

Here is a list of productivity vampires with some very specific suggestions on how to improve in each of these categories by taking specific action. Keep in mind that the more you're able to control and manage the forces against you that are sucking away your productivity, the more successful you will be in achieving your goals and your dreams. Productivity vampires can happen both at work and at home.

### 1. E-mail

I work with a lot of clients across the country, and particularly with those that are in executive leadership positions. What I find is that a lot of people in the world of business are completely overwhelmed and buried in massive amounts of e-mails. This comes in the form of reading them, responding to them, and writing them. Many people that I talk to in the world of business are telling me that they're getting between 600 and 800 e-mails *per day*. I was quite amazed and shocked by that number, and what they tell me is they can never really ever get caught up because of the stunning amount of information that they are getting bombarded with on a daily basis. *What to do about it*—I think there are several things you can do to make your e-mail much more productive, and the biggest part of it is how you *handle* your e-mail.

- **Color coding for priority**—In many e-mail systems, you have the unique ability to color code whom the e-mail is from. So, for example, if I have a boss I can designate in the settings of my e-mail system that the e-mails that come from my boss will be in a certain color like red. The advantage of this is that when I go to look at my e-mail, I could respond to the ones that are from my boss first. Secondly, you can designate that all e-mails that are sent to you directly are color-coded in blue. I can then designate answering the ones in red first, the ones in blue second. Further, if you color code the ones on which you are cc'd in a different color (let's say black), you can choose to answer those last, because they were not sent to you directly, you were only copied, and you may or may not ever get to them. They are of low priority. This gives you an instant way of prioritizing what should be responded to first.

- **Handle once**—Many people will open an e-mail and read it, and then they will close it and not respond. They will then go back later, read it again, and not respond. This means you literally have looked at the same e-mail perhaps 5 to 6 times before actually responding. I recommend reading the e-mail and either responding to or deleting it at that time. To be clear, there are instances when you need some time to reflect on a specific e-mail before you respond in a thoughtful way. But the general rule should be to try to handle each e-mail only once.

- **Pick up the phone**—If you end up e-mailing someone back and forth more than two times, trying to clarify information, then please just pick up the phone and call them. This will save you a tremendous amount of time and energy because a five-minute phone call can, I believe, save you an hour of e-mailing back and forth. Besides, with e-mail there can be a lot of misinterpretation and confusion about what something actually means.

- **Block out time for "like" activities**—One technique I think that will massively improve your productivity is to block out e-mail time. What I mean by that is to block out an hour to just send and receive e-mails, and don't do anything else at that time. Unfortunately, what happens in most cases is that someone sends an e-mail, or is reading an e-mail, and their phone rings. They answer the phone and get into a conversation for a short time before hanging up and returning to e-mail, but they can't remember what it was that they were writing or reading. Then it takes a long time to get back into the groove. If you can be disciplined enough to restrict your time to only e-mailing or phone calling or working on projects, the thought processes will be clearer.

## 2. Phone calls and voice mail

I find it interesting that many people seem to believe that if the phone rings, they have to actually answer it at that time. Someone can be in the middle of a meeting, or in the middle of answering an important e-mail, and will stop and answer the phone. This, again, is a great interruption and distraction to your time and productivity. What I highly recommend is to let phone calls go to voice mail and then return them all in one block of time. Constantly having to answer the phone interrupts what it is that you're doing. Let me be clear about one thing—obviously, if your CEO or your biggest customer on the whole planet calls you, it might be a smart idea to answer the phone if you're available. But if it's anyone else calling, you may want to defer answering the phone and put all the phone calls that are returned into one block of time, making you more productive and less distracted.

There is no rule anywhere that says you have to answer the phone when it rings—it's not a school bell, you're not Pavlov's dog—and if you want to be productive, you need to start doing things just a little bit differently, not like everybody else.

### 3. Environmental distractions

There are many environmental distractions that can happen both at work and at home. These distractions can be 1) visual, 2) verbal, 3) noise, or 4) internal. Let's examine each.

#### Visual

In my opinion, the state of the modern workplace is unfortunately designed to create way too many visual distractions for somebody who is trying to focus on their work. I've seen many examples of this while traveling around the country doing training and speaking. The first example that I have seen is the extremely popular trend of the open office environment. This consists of just a series of long flat tables with no cubes, walls, and offices, and everyone works in *one common space*. I personally find this enormously distracting from a visual standpoint because there are very many things going on around you; it's very easy to get distracted. It's almost as if architects have created an office version of attention deficit disorder. Most people who are working in the open office environment have to put on headsets to block out the noise that is created in the open office environments. Unfortunately, this does not eliminate the visual distractions because all day long every worker sees a bunch of people walking around trying to do the various activities involved with their work. The second example that I have seen, which is gaining popularity, is conference rooms that have all four walls that are clear glass. People in a meeting, no matter in what direction they look, can see activity outside of the conference room, and that is distracting. I once did training in a beautiful meeting room in Laguna Beach, California, and the designer who designed the meeting room made sure that the front wall of the room was clear glass with no curtains. Unfortunately, outside the room (which was on the second floor) was a beautiful scenic view of the ocean and, to make it even more distracting, volleyball courts where people in bikinis were playing volleyball! How in the world can we expect people to pay attention in a meeting when they're looking out at the ocean? So what can you do about this? Obviously, if you work for a company, you do not have the power to control the architectural design of the offices, but there are certain things that you can do to limit your distractions visually. First of all, if you have the ability to go to a private space (like a conference room or even a quiet corner), then you can block out the visual distractions. Secondly, if you're working on an important project, you may ask your manager whether you may work from home. Often in my career when I was working in corporate America, if I was working on an important project, I asked my boss if I could work from home and he would let me do that. I found that I was tremendously more productive working at home than I was in a noisy, interruption-filled office. If you are fortunate enough to work in a cube or an office, try to set up your desk to face away from visual distractions so that you will not be distracted by people walking by your cube or office. Thirdly, when you are working on a project or something that you need to focus or concentrate on, be sure to turn off all notifications on e-mails and also avoid the temptation to look at your display on your phone when your phone rings. Make a list of the items that you find distracting and try to engineer ways of working around them. For example, if looking out the window is enormously distracting, pull the shades or blinds so you won't be distracted. It is up to you to control whatever you can in order to be as productive as possible.

### Verbal

The problem with verbal distractions is it is very easy to get caught up in accidentally listening to what other people are saying and then have your train of thought completely derailed. In the open office environment, verbal distractions are obviously an occupational hazard because no matter which way you turn in your work area, there are people beside you and in front of you, all talking. Sometimes they are talking to each other, sometimes they are talking to someone on the phone, and sometimes they are talking to you, which ends up being an interruption. One thing I have noticed lately is if I am traveling by train or by plane, it's very easy to be overwhelmed with the cacophony of everyone conversing on their cell phones. On trains it seems as if everybody is involved with conversation on their cell phone. On planes everyone seems to be on their cell phone until the flight attendants insist that they turn them off. What can we do to make sure that we're not subjected to verbal distractions? If you think of verbal distractions as being an audio channel, then what we have to do is somehow mechanically change the channel. So the most obvious solution is to use earphones to block out or reduce the noise. With earphones you have two options: you can either listen to music to block out the noise or some headphones even have the option of creating white noise that will block out the sound as well. The other way to block out the verbal distractions is to work from a different location, be it a conference room, another office, or your home.

### Noise

Sometimes there is noise that can be a distraction, and it is not verbal, but just noise. As a professional speaker, I've often been speaking in meeting rooms, when suddenly outside the room, people in the hotel would begin doing some form of construction, so you could hear jackhammers or other construction equipment. I have also been speaking many times in a room where someone outside was mowing the lawn or trimming hedges and/or using leaf blowers, which was extremely distracting. I can literally look into the audience and see people being massively distracted by the noise from somewhere outside the room. I once spoke at a meeting at a hotel where the wall of the meeting room was a shared wall with a train station that was just next door. What I found extremely amusing about the meeting room was that at least once in each hour the room would shake violently (because the train was literally on the tracks next door) and you would also hear the noise of the train and at times the loud train whistle. As a speaker, I had done my research on the room, and I knew the timetable of the train, so when the train arrived I just stopped speaking for about 45 seconds to let it pass, because I realized that no one would hear me speaking during that time. I didn't really understand why a hotel would have a meeting room that was literally attached by one wall to a train station, but I had to figure out how I could control it myself by at least stopping while the train was passing. I want you to be consciously aware of what noises distract you, and use tools that will reduce or eliminate the noise so that you can continue to think clearly. Don't let yourself be distracted and your productivity ruined by external noise.

### Internal

With everyone so busy these days, I think it is very easy to get internally distracted, which can lead to a reduction of productivity. The question is, what causes someone to be internally distracted? Sometimes we can be internally distracted by external factors such as a room being too hot or too cold. We can also be distracted through physical discomfort, as when the chair that we are sitting in is uncomfortable, or when the room is too bright because of the sunlight streaming in through a window or too dark so we can't quite see clearly. When you are distracted by external factors, your thinking gets muddled. The other element that can distract us is thinking about one thing while we were trying to do another. For example, you may be working on a project, and as you are writing the project report some other idea comes up, and instead of dismissing that idea, you start thinking about it although it is not related to what you're working on at all. So, essentially, you've created your own distraction by letting your thoughts go off the rails. So how do we solve the problem of internal distraction? One of the things we can do is to try to make sure that we are physically comfortable. If you are too hot or cold, try to change the physical space to make it more comfortable. If you're sitting in an uncomfortable chair or at an uncomfortable desk, try to change the space that you are working in. While working, try as much as possible to keep your thoughts focused on what you are working on and not allow yourself to get distracted. One technique that I think is very useful (to avoid getting distracted) is to work from an outline or a series of notes that will help you stay focused. Secondly, I think it is a good idea to occasionally take breaks to get up and stretch and walk around. You'll find that when you return to the work you will be a lot more focused and not as distracted. Thirdly, try to discover when you are most productive doing specific types of work. For example, I have discovered that I'm much more productive in writing in the morning hours when my mind is fresh than late at night when my mind might be a little more fatigued. However, in contrast, some people may find that they are night owls—they do their best work late in the evening. Give some thought to when you are at your most productive so that you can actually schedule the work that you're doing at the time that you will be most effective and productive.

## Boss

Depending on the kind of boss you report to, your boss may be either a productivity vampire or a helpful driver to your productivity. I certainly hope that your boss belongs to the second type and not the first. The reality is some bosses end up being a mix of the two. Sometimes, bosses can be helpful in terms of productivity, and sometimes they can be a hindrance. One of the things that I've noticed about most people in terms of working with their boss is that they do not negotiate with the boss in terms of projects and time frames. If a boss comes into someone's work area and says, "I need this right away," because they have a good work ethic, they say, "Sure, I'll get to that right away." The problem is that they don't ask for any clarification on what "right away" means. Does it mean immediately? Does it mean by the end of the day? Does it mean by the end of the week? So I believe one extremely helpful technique you can use is to ask exactly when they need it. I don't think there is anything wrong with actually negotiating with your boss. For example when your boss assigns a project there is nothing wrong with saying, "Sure, I'd be happy to work on that, but just a quick question for you. Based on the list of projects that I'm working on, which project would you like me to delay or defer in order to work on this one?" This does two things: first of all, it lets your boss know what it is you're actually working on, and it allows you to force them (in a subtle way) to make a decision as to what it is you're going to work on next. So if done properly, it's perfectly okay to negotiate with your boss in order to be more productive.

### 4. Social media

Let's face it, almost everyone on the planet is deeply involved in social media. It may be involvement with Facebook, Twitter, Instagram, Pinterest, YouTube, and a whole range of other social media channels. I'm not talking about social media being used professionally for marketing or networking, but about social media when used socially, as it can certainly be a productivity vampire. It is so easy to log on to Facebook to read people's postings, and to then respond to what they posted, and before you know it, you've literally consumed two hours of your time that disappeared into the social media abyss. You look at the clock and you cannot believe that you've lost two hours. The other question that I always think about is, what did you actually achieve? The problem with social media is it's very much like chocolate: it's pleasurable while you're eating it, but what do you have when you're done? Unfortunately, the answer at the end of that time is "nothing." I don't believe that a year from now anyone will be able to remember what you posted or what anyone else posted to Facebook or any other social media. So my caution is that while you're at work and while you are at home, be sure to very carefully budget how much time you spend on social media. If you're going to use social media as a way of unwinding after a tough day, put a time limit on how much time you spend there.

### 5. The Internet

The Internet is a great place to research and find valuable information and resources. On the other hand, it also can be a very dangerous vampire for your productivity because it is very easy to endlessly surf the Net for hours at a time and not be productive except for watching the cutest puppy dog video you've ever seen. Surfing the Internet and spending your time randomly looking at websites, following links from those websites, and looking at those websites is a tangled web that is very tempting and will suck up all of your productivity time professionally and personally. I know that it can be highly entertaining to see what Grumpy Cat is up to, but the question is how is that going to help you be more productive in your life? I'm not asking you to never take a break at home or at work, but just advising you to control it.

## 6. Procrastination

All of us at one time in our lives or another have been guilty of procrastination. What is procrastination? I believe that it really is *deciding* to do something that's more fun because you're avoiding doing something that's less fun. In other words, it's more pleasurable for you to do some other activity than actually working on the things you're procrastinating doing. In terms of productivity, procrastination actually is a great drain on your productivity for a few very important reasons: 1) When you procrastinate, it means that you're delaying doing something that may be important. What I have generally found is that the longer you delay in doing something, the less effective you are because you have to remember exactly what it is that you're supposed to be working on. Let's say you have a meeting as part of a project team and you have certain things that you're assigned to do. Let's also say that you procrastinate and you wait several weeks before you start on your assigned task. When you go back to your notes, because it has been several weeks it's much harder to remember what it is that you're supposed to do, and it takes you much longer to get back into the groove, remembering what it is you're supposed to do. However, in the opposite example, if you start working on your actions a few days after the meeting you will certainly have a lot more clarity about the specific activities that you've been assigned to complete. 2) Procrastination will also often end up costing you money. A friend of mine bought a brand-new phone from a large phone retailer, and the phone came with a $100 rebate. The companies that make cell phones never make the rebate an instant rebate; they make it a mail-in rebate. I have also noticed that mail-in rebates often have multiple steps that you have to follow in order to send the rebate in, including copying receipts, copying UPC codes from various packaging, and filling out a simple form, right? Oh no—that would make it easy—instead what they do is make you fill out a very complicated form. My friend knew the rebate had to be sent in within a 60-day time period from the date of purchase. Because it was such a painful, monotonous, and arduous task, he continued to put it off day after day. Of course, I'm sure you can guess the rest of the story: he ended up going past the 60-day time requirement and was denied a rebate, which meant that he lost $100. So procrastination usually ends up costing us money by causing us to miss deadlines and/or be charged late fees and penalties. 3) I also think procrastination creates an emotional toll. When people procrastinate, even though it brings them short-term pleasure to do so, it ends up costing them emotionally because they feel bad for procrastinating. When they procrastinate enough, they start participating in negative self-talk, which makes them feel even worse. So don't subject yourself to the downward emotional spiral of continuous procrastination, because all it really does is make you feel bad. 4) I have seen many cases where procrastination also leads to a poorer quality result. Let's face it, when someone has to rush a project because they have procrastinated, in most cases it will not be of the same quality as if they had spent more time working on it in a reasonable time frame. I remember as a child procrastinating on a science class project that I was working on and trying to complete it at the last minute right before the deadline. I don't remember the grade I got on that project, but I do remember realizing that it could've been done much better.

### *7. Lack of preparation*

It almost seems counterintuitive to say, but lack of preparation is a productivity vampire. The reality is that just a small investment in preparation will make you considerably more productive. I have always believed that proper preparation reduces trepidation. When you attend a meeting and you are prepared, you're much more confident and less anxious about what may happen in the meeting. When you're not prepared, you will have less confidence and you certainly will be more anxious about how the meeting is going to go. Let me give you an example. If I buy something for my house that requires assembly, I can take everything out of the box and dump everything on the floor and start assembling. However, if I take 10 minutes and carefully stage all the materials that I'm going to need to do the job, and I go and get all the tools that I need to do the job, and I go through all the instructions before I start, I'm much more likely to be successful because I did 10 minutes of preparation.

# WORK IT!

How much time do you spend a day on leisure activities?

_____

_____

_____

How much time do you spend a day watching TV?

_____

_____

_____

How do you feel about those numbers?

_____

_____

_____

What time management system do you use now?

_____

_____

_____

_____

_____

What do you like about it?

_____
_____
_____
_____

What do you dislike about it?

_____
_____
_____
_____

Where can you be more productive?

_____
_____
_____
_____

What are the productivity vampires in your life? What can you do about them?

_____
_____
_____
_____

## CHAPTER FOUR

### *JOLT #4*
# PLANNING IS THE KEY TO MASSIVE PRODUCTIVITY

## PLANNING FOR MAXIMUM SUCCESS

*"Plans are nothing; planning is everything."*
—DWIGHT D. EISENHOWER

As we have grown up, we have heard many sayings about planning—"Fail to plan and plan to fail." "I love it when a plan comes together." There are a lot of ideas about planning in the world. Most people believe that it is important to plan, but most people do not plan well at all. My wife and I were recently driving down a country road and noticed the traffic was backed up for miles, and we assumed that there was an accident somewhere ahead. When we finally got to the bottleneck where cars were backed up for miles, we discovered the true reason for the delay: a tractor-trailer truck driver had run out of gas and was stalled in one lane. The reason we knew he had run out of gas is he was filling up his tanks with large gas cans in order to have enough to make it to the nearest gas station. We both found it amazing that a *professional* truck driver would run out of gas—talk about poor planning!

If you want to be massively successful and massively productive (and I do believe that the two are related), then you have to start planning for maximum success. If someone decided to go hiking on the Appalachian Trail for 6 to 9 months, it certainly would be a good idea for them to plan their journey. If they did not plan their journey, they could end up running out of food and water on their adventure. If they didn't bring the appropriate items for the trip, they could be either too cold or too hot.

So in order to be more productive, spend more time planning, because the more time you spend planning, the more productive you will be.

## THE BEGINNING PART OF THE PROCESS

Using the example again of the hike on the Appalachian Trail, I think the beginning question would be, what is your goal? Your answer, as a reasonable person, would probably be to hike the entire length of the Appalachian Trail and to reach the destination by a certain date. That, obviously, would be your goal. So as we discussed in several chapters, the first thing to do is to be as specific as possible about your goal.

In my mind, for your goal to be successful you need to have the following:

### Measurement

How would you know that you are successful if you couldn't measure it? For example, if you want to be a best-selling author, which certainly sounds like a noble goal, the question is, how many copies of the book would you need to sell in order to be a best-selling author?

### The time element

Obviously, if you set a goal it would be a good idea to come up with a time element as part of your goal. For example, if I'm working on a financial goal for my business, I would want to reach a certain amount of revenue by the end of the second quarter. So I may write down "to reach $10 million in revenue by the end of quarter two."

### As specific as possible

For example, if you write down a goal of "lose weight in the next three months," that goal is not specific enough. What you need to say is "lose 19 pounds in the next three months and reduce the measurement of my waist size by 4 inches." This goal would be much more specific.

There are many schools of thought out there that believe goals should contain many other elements such as being 1) achievable and 2) realistic. I am not fond of using the metric of *achievable* on goals because I think it limits people's thinking in terms of goal achievement. I also personally don't care for the use of the word *realistic*, because I often think it is used by people who want to be negative. Often, if a dreamer who has big ideas brings up a good idea, the negative people of the world will say, "Come on, you need to be more *realistic*." I don't really know or understand what "realistic" means because most people do think way too small. To me, the people of the world that are most successful are those who think big.

## THE ELEMENTS OF PLANNING

So once we have nailed down our goals and have them in writing, we want to apply the planning to achieve them. I don't think that you can plan if you don't know what it is you're planning for. So the centerpiece for our planning has to be a goal orientation.

So I believe the first element of planning is to look at time increments. I believe those increments can be as follows:

- Short term – In my definition, that means 4 to 6 months.

- Mid term – In my definition, that means 6 to 12 months.

- Long term – In my definition, that means 12 to 18 months.

If I am planning on achieving a specific goal, I can then take that goal and break it into short-term, mid-term, and long-term goals. That in itself is fairly simple.

The next thing you need to look at is categories for planning. What do I mean by categories? What I mean by categories is all the elements that you need to look at that need to be part of the plan. Let's say, for example, I decided I'm going to build a brand-new office for my company. When I look at the aspects of building a brand-new office, I might look at the following categories (I call this RPM, as in generating greater horsepower):

### Resources

What resources will I need on this particular project to ensure that I will be successful? The list of resources could include an architect, a general contractor, an interior designer, a project manager, suppliers, vendors, and partners.

## People

What people will I need internally and externally to successfully pull off this project? When I mentioned resources, I was referring to specific roles that someone would fill such as an architect or a general contractor. But if you run an organization, the question is what people you want to have involved in the project to manage it, or be part of it, or contribute to it, or generate ideas for it. So those would be the people that would help you with the project in some way, shape, or form to ensure that it is successful.

## Materials

What materials will I need in order to complete this project? If I am building an office, I might need real estate, building materials, permits, furniture, artwork, carpets, rugs, and interior décor. This of course always depends on who is providing what, and who is buying what.

The RPM model simply helps create categories of things you need to look at in order to make sure that you're not forgetting something on any initiative that you take. Here is another important point that I want to make—it is absolutely essential that all this goes down on paper or electronically in writing. Why would that be important? Because, obviously, if you work on an important initiative you will need to be constantly going back and referring to information that you have, and the more complex the project, the more successful you will be if everything is in writing.

If you take a look at construction managers who manage large construction projects, they always have a *written plan* that includes all the steps involved in getting the project completed. This helps them constantly stay on track in order to be successful and on time with completion of the project.

So I strongly recommend that you make a list of the resources, people, and materials that you need to be successful in your planning.

## PROJECT PLAN

I believe that once you have identified your goals and objectives, and your goals are following the necessary guidelines, the next step is to create a project plan. For a project plan, go to the end of the project (meaning the end date) and then work backward from there. So, for example, if you are working on an initiative and need to be done six months from now, you would go to the calendar, and using the date of six months from now, work your way backward to determine what you need to do each month, each week, and each day.

You then create a written document that shows all the items as they relate to the calendar. You can then take all these benchmarks and enter them into your time management system electronically or in writing. The idea behind putting all these activities and benchmarks into your time management system is that your time management system will then remind you on a daily, weekly, and monthly basis what you need to do to be successful and complete your initiative.

Your project plan can simply be something as simple as a regular old calendar where you write in the specific dates, an electronic time management system that will continually remind you electronically when things are due, or if you have an extremely complex project you can use project management software specifically made for managing large, complex projects.

Stumbling blocks to look out for when planning include:

### Not having a plan

I am quite amazed by how many people I talk to as I travel around the country who tell me they want to do something. When I ask them when and how they're going to do it, they just give me a blank look. This clearly tells me that they do not have a plan, don't plan to have a plan, and are literally clueless. How can you achieve anything if you do not have a plan? I know that people can sometimes be successful without planning, but that is just dumb luck. There are people who stumble into success despite themselves, and they just happen to hit the right thing at the right time despite the fact that they don't have a plan. This, unfortunately, gives them the mistaken notion that they can be successful without planning, and that is an invitation to disaster.

### Having someone else's plan

If you want to be, as I call it, "the architect of your own life," it is very important not to follow other people's plans for your life and your work but to follow your own plan for your life and your work. As I have often said, "If you do not have a plan, one will be provided for you and will not be your own; it'll be someone else's," and it will be to their benefit, not necessarily yours.

### Making the plan too vague

The problem I see with many people in terms of the planning is their plans are too vague. If your plans are too vague, you can't achieve them because you don't know what they are. Often as I travel around the country, because I am a book author people feel compelled to tell me that they would like to write a book. When they tell me that they want to write a book, I usually get excited for them and ask them what they plan to write about. In most cases the answer is "I'm not sure what I want to write about; I just know that I want to write a book." This is like saying, "I know that I want a boat; I just don't know what kind, how big, and why I want one."

### Having a plan that is not time bound

All plans need to be time bound. In my opinion, there are two elements of the plan that need to be time bound: 1) We need benchmarks along the way that tell us that we are making the progress that we are supposed to be making. For example, if we have a 16-week plan, we should know where we should be in week two in order to achieve the 16-week objective. 2) We should also have an end date on which we intend to be totally and completely done. If you do not have time in your plan, it is not a plan but a vague wish. As I often say to groups that I speak to, in order to be successful you have to prioritize, agendasize, and calendarize. The idea behind having a plan that is time bound is to make sure that it has been calendarized.

### It must be in writing

I have people tell me all the time that they have plans, but the plans are in their head and not in writing. In my opinion, one requirement of any plan is it needs to be written so you can refer to it on a regular and consistent basis to track where you are. I also find that when things are in writing, they are much clearer and easier to track, and it is much easier to show them to others and to review them with other people as well. It's hard for me to show you a thought in my head. It's very easy for me to show you a project plan that is in writing.

# WORK IT!

What is your biggest strength when it comes to planning?

_____

_____

_____

_____

What is your biggest area for improvement? Why?

_____

_____

_____

_____

When working on a project, do you create a project plan?

_____

_____

_____

_____

Have you ever thought about the RPM model before?

_____

_____

_____

_____

In terms of planning, what do you need to do more often?

_____

_____

Why?

# CHAPTER FIVE

## *JOLT #5*
## KNOW WHAT TIME OF DAY YOU'RE AT YOUR BEST

### NIGHT OWL OR EARLY BIRD: LOOKING AT WHEN YOU ARE MOST PRODUCTIVE

*"I'm a morning person because I learned to write my novels while still practicing law. I would get to the office at 6:30 A.M. and write until other people arrived, around 9. Now I still do that. I start at 6:30 or 7, and I'll write until 11, then take an hour off, then work until about 2 p.m. By then my brain has had enough."*
—STEVE BERRY

To begin this chapter I thought it might be useful to share an article I wrote for *Inc.* This article may help you think a little differently about how you start your day. The article is "5 Easy Morning Habits That Can Make Your Day More Productive."

93

Do you want to be more productive? Do you want to be more motivated today? Happier? Then put some thought into the most important part of the day—how the day starts. I know it may seem obvious, but the beginning of your day is the same as the beginning of a race—if the runner stumbles at the starting line, it's hard to get caught up. I don't think many people think about the start of their day; they just fall into a habit or routine. Here are five ways to jumpstart your day.

### Get up one hour earlier

Get up earlier so your morning can be a mindful way to start your day and you have time to actually think about your day and not get caught up in the fire drill. This is a great way to start your day because it is also more relaxing, not having to rush around like a crazy person. People who are successful set aside time to think about what they are doing.

### Start with only positive content

Many people get up in the morning and turn on the news as they are getting ready for their day. While that sounds like a great idea, the problem is you're starting off the day with very negative content. Let's face it, the news is full of bad news—death, fires, terrorism, and tragedy. I recently watched a woman on a morning flight on her laptop watching all the news about the latest shooting tragedy. She literally spent two hours of her time reading all about murder. I don't stand in judgment, but why would anyone want to start their day that way? Think about changing your morning habits, and instead start with something positive—read a positive book or useful article online, watch a positive video like a TED Talk, subscribe to a thought-provoking blog, read something spiritual, pray, or meditate. Think of it as your morning ritual for results.

### Take a few moments to journal

Take a few moments during the quiet time of the morning before anyone is up and about to write down your goals, objectives, dreams, and ambitions. Reflect on where you are and where you are going. Remind yourself why you're working so hard. People say it's not just about the destination but the journey, but it's important to continually remind yourself where the destination is, because it can be very motivating. Journaling really helps cement your thinking.

### Do something to raise your energy level

In order to jumpstart your day, you need to make sure that you have a high level of energy to work with. Think about what activities would give you the most energy for your day. Doing an aerobic or anaerobic workout can help you be more energetic, and having a nice healthy breakfast can help you feel more energetic; or you can listen to high-energy music or take a hot shower or have breakfast with your kids and your spouse and talk about their day. There are no correct answers about raising your energy level except knowing what works for you. What raises your energy?

### Plan your day in writing

Take a few moments and plan your day in writing, making an action list of the three to four essential things that you need to get done today, both professionally and personally. You can't hit a target if you don't know what it is. The action list gives you a track to run on. Get on track early.

I think John Wayne said it best about starting your day: "Tomorrow is the most important thing in life. Comes into us at midnight very clean. It's perfect when it arrives and it puts itself in our hands. It hopes we've learned something from yesterday."

Here is an important critical question I want you to think about: When are you most productive? Are you more productive in the morning? Are you more productive in the afternoon? Are you more productive in the evening?

I think that one of the essential elements of productivity is thinking about when you do your best work, at what time, and then arranging your work around that awareness and realization. I think it's interesting that some people have never really given this much thought and have never really analyzed when they're at their best.

Here are some questions that I think will help you think more clearly about when you are most productive:

### Question #1—Are you an early bird?

Many people who like to get up early in the morning are referred to as early birds, early risers, or morning persons. How can you tell if you're an early bird or an early morning person? I personally think that it is a matter of what you like, and how you feel. If you are the kind of person that loves (and I do mean loves) getting up early, right when the sun comes up or even before, and doing all of your most important tasks early in the morning, then you are probably someone who is an early riser. Another great litmus test of whether you're an early riser or not is whether you would wake up early even if you did not set the clock. I meet many people who say, "Even if I tried to sleep in, I would wake up anyway." So using those definitions, decide whether you are an early bird or not.

### Question #2—Are you a night owl?

Some people refer to people who are night owls as late nighters, or night owls. These are the people who actually love staying up late, and the later they stay up, the more energy they have. It would not be uncharacteristic for them to actually stay up till one or two o'clock in the morning and enjoy it. These are the folks that have the most energy in the evening and find that they are at the most creative when they are working in the later hours of the day. A great test of whether you're a night owl or not is how late would you stay up if you didn't have to get up the next day? If you don't have to get up the next day and you stay up until early in the morning hours, you probably are a night owl.

I am not suggesting that you're not capable of changing from one to the other. For example, if I am on a business trip and I have to get up extremely early in the morning in order to travel to a place where I am going to speak early in the morning, I'm still going to have to get up early, regardless of whether I'm a night owl or a morning person. If I am traveling on business and my flight is canceled or delayed and I end up taking a very late-night flight that lands somewhere at one o'clock in the morning, I still have to do it whether I'm a night owl or not.

So what is the point of this thought process about being either an early bird or a night owl? It is deciding what kind of work you want to do and *when you do it.*

In the ideal world, you would want to try to shift certain kinds of work you do to the time when you are at *your physical and mental peak* state and when you believe you are able to do your best work. I call this your maximum productivity zone (MPZ).

Let's say, for example, I am a salesperson, and I work for a company representing a product and selling it across the region. If I am an early morning person, I would want to think about the following:

### *The critically important tasks*

If I am an early riser, I would want to take my most important sales tasks and try to put them into the morning hours when I am "at my best" and have my highest level of energy. I want those tasks in the MPZ zone. So if I am a sales professional, some of the most important tasks that I may do in the morning hours would be:

#### Sales calls to existing customers

In person or by phone.

#### Brainstorming sales solutions

If this is the time of day when I am at my highest level of creativity, that's when I would probably want to work on brainstorming sales solutions.

#### Working on sales proposals

If this is when I am at my most mentally sharp, this is when I would probably want to work on sales proposals.

#### Prospecting

If I have my highest level of energy in the morning hours, this is probably when I want to do most of my sales prospecting.

#### Follow-up

If I need to follow up on existing sales proposals in order to close those pieces of business, I probably want to try to do those when I am at my best—again, in the early morning.

I certainly think that at this point you get the idea—in order to be more productive, I want to shift the most important things that I do to the MPZ morning hours if I am a morning person because that's when I can probably be the most effective.

So, then, here is the critical question: If I am this morning person and I am in sales, what can I do in the afternoon? In the afternoon, I could do some of the least important tasks for a salesperson:

### Administrative reports

I have certain administrative reports that I have to do on a regular basis, and maybe I do those in the afternoon instead of in the morning.

### Filing

If I have various filings that need to be done, I can do those in the afternoon.

### Meetings with internal staff

I can have meetings with internal staff in the afternoon instead of in the morning, thereby not cutting into my sales time.

## *Maintenance*

Things like ordering samples, scheduling appointments, working through logistics, and making travel arrangements could all be done during the maintenance portion of the day.

You get the idea. Once you figure out when you are at your best, you're going to try to shift the work to those times when you can be more productive. My wife Rachael, for example, is most definitely a morning person. When she gets up in the morning and starts working, she can be massively productive in the morning hours and in the early afternoon. Here is what she has learned about herself—when she gets into the late evening hours, her productivity goes down dramatically, so she is much better off doing more mundane tasks in the evening hours instead of trying to do the intellectually challenging tasks then. She has learned she's much better off waiting until the next morning to do them because she can do them three or four times faster if she waits until morning.

## THE BENEFITS OF TIME SHIFTING
## TASKS TO YOUR MPZ:

### *You will get more done*

I believe that when most people are working in their MPZ, they are probably four or five times more productive than they are if they are working at times when they're not in the MPZ.

### *You will get better results*

I think that when you are in the zone, you will not only be more productive in terms of getting more work done, but I also think the quality of your work will be better. I think everybody knows when they're "in the zone" how that feels, and when they feel that way they do better work.

### *You will feel better about the work*

Sometimes when you're working on a project and you feel like you're off or not in the zone and you feel like you're struggling to get it done, it is not a good feeling. When you're in the MPZ and you feel like you're firing on all cylinders, it is a great feeling and you feel much better about the work.

### *You can make easier decisions*

When you are deciding when to work on something, you can decide whether to work on something in your zone or on something not in your zone. If someone contacts you and asks for a meeting with you, you can also use your MPZ preference to decide when the best time to meet would be. If you're a morning person and need to be sharp, and someone wants to meet with you and it is a critically important meeting, then try to convince them to meet in the morning and not in the afternoon.

### Your credibility will be enhanced

Your credibility will be enhanced because when you work more in the zone, all the things that are listed above will improve, and the quality of your work will be perceived as being more credible and of higher quality.

I want to make sure that you understand that I do practice realism. I do appreciate that at times you have to schedule different activities when they may not be to your convenience. However, when you have a choice, try to schedule things when you can be at your highest level of productivity, creativity, and efficiency.

## WORKING WITH OTHER PEOPLE

### The boss

If you have someone that you report to, try to figure out whether they are a morning bird or a night owl. Obviously, one of the things you want to try to do is determine which one they are and you want to be strategic about when you meet with them. If I am meeting with my boss and I want them to be at their sharpest, I would obviously try to set up a meeting with them when they are at their best based on their own individual MPZ. If, on the other hand, what we are meeting about is not as critical, then we can decide that we may want to meet with them during their non-MPZ time. I just want you to be cognizant as to when it is for them. Many years ago when I worked in corporate America, I had a boss that was definitely a morning person, so whenever I met with him I tried as much as possible to make sure that it was a morning meeting, and for him the earlier the better.

### The team

If you have a team of people who work with you, you can use the same strategic approach to determine when the best time to meet with them would be, by analyzing their time preferences—whether they are night owls or morning birds. You can do this through observation or by asking them what time of day they feel they're more productive.

## YOUR PRODUCTIVITY ENVIRONMENT

We have talked about what time of day (a.m. or p.m.) you're most productive. But now we address the question of whether it is possible that you have a productivity environment that is most useful for you, when you are at your best.

I talk to people who constantly tell me that it is impossible for them to get any work done because the environment that they work in is subject to constant and endless interruptions throughout the day. So the only time they can actually get anything done is if they come in early or stay late. Obviously, this is extremely counterproductive in every way because we are allowing other people to control our productivity.

So here are some thoughts about your productivity environment that you definitely might want to consider:

### In terms of space, where do you feel that you are most productive?

When you analyze space, where are you most productive in terms of space? If you work for a company, is it in your office? If you work for yourself, is it in your home office or at your local Starbucks or in a conference room at an office facility where you can rent space? Is it sitting in seat 11A on a coast-to-coast flight? I want you to give great thought to the kind of spaces where you're able to be the most productive.

### In terms of space, where are the areas where you feel least productive?

Looking at the times when we are not productive at all, what do you think are the times when you are least productive in terms of space? The question to ask yourself is why you're not productive in that space. Is it visual distractions? Is it auditory distractions (otherwise known as noise)? Is it other people distractions (many people who are coming in and constantly interrupting you)? You need to not only analyze the space that is the least productive but to also identify what it is about those spaces that makes you least productive. If you're able to do that, you might be able to turn a space that is least productive into one that is perhaps more productive by fixing some of the elements that are distracting you and causing you not to focus. Many people that I talk to have an office that has a door, and they complain that they're constantly being interrupted. My response is "what would happen if you closed the door and asked people not to disturb you for a certain amount of time?" Often people tell me they didn't think of that idea, because they did not want to be rude or be viewed as inaccessible. But the reality is, I think, that it is okay to have times when you're not available and are not accessible. So figure out what adjustments you can make to eliminate the barriers that make you less productive in that particular space.

### In terms of space, is the space that you normally work in set up in a way to maximize your productivity?

When we look at workspaces, we realize that sometimes workspaces are set up to maximize productivity for that individual person and that sometimes they're not set up to maximize productivity at all—instead, they are set up to diminish productivity. For example, someone I met recently in a meeting that I was conducting told me that their office had two doors. One door to their office was the door that *everyone* entering the department had to go through, and they all had to walk by his desk in order to go into other departments. The other door led to another meeting room where several other people worked, so people were constantly going in and out of the doors all day long. If your desk is located in the middle of Grand Central Station, you're probably not going to be as productive as you would like to be. In her book, *Organize Your Business,* Rachael Doyle (yes, as a side note, that is my wife) wrote about some ideas about setting up your desk in order to maximize your productivity. Here is what she had to say that I think you'll find helpful:

### Idea #1—Welcome to the desk zone

Take a careful look at your zones in your office. What do I mean by zones? I want you to imagine that there is a huge round target with three rings that you could lay over the top of your desk area. Ring one in zone A—this is the zone where everything is within reach of your arm. Next would be the second ring, which I will call zone B. This is the area that would require you to roll your chair a few feet away in order to grab something. Then we have zone C, which would be the outer ring, an area that you would have to get up out of your chair and walk over to in order to get something you need to use. Here is the problem— most people never really analyze what items should be in zones A, B, or C; they just kind of happened by accident. So someone may have something to use all of the time, but they have to get up out of their chair to go grab it. Someone may have something they hardly ever use, and it's within their arm's length to grab. This consumes a lot of time, and tends to be frustrating for the person sitting at the desk, which is you.

### Idea #2—It's a zone defense

Decide what items go in zone A. I obviously don't know what it is that you do for a living, but I'm going to guess that there are certain things that should definitely be in your zone A that are literally at your fingertips: 1) a computer, 2) a monitor, 3) a printer, 4) something to write on, 5) something to write with, 6) supplies such as staplers, paperclips, etc., and 7) a wastebasket. The problem is that some people have items in zone A that they hardly ever use, and some people have items in zone C that they use all the time. So take some time to analyze which items you use all the time (every hour, every few hours, or every day), and put those items in zone A. Then decide which items go in zone B and which items in zone C. I used to work for a company, and every time I needed to print out a document, I had to walk down a long hallway, which was about as long as half of a football field. This was a tremendous waste of time and very inefficient, and led to walking back and forth all day long collecting things that I printed out on my printer.

### Idea #3—Do a clutter audit

Take a few hours, and, sitting in your desk area, decide the items that are absolutely nonessential for you to do your job effectively. I find that once people have been in an organization for a long time, they end up with a large collection of tchotchkes on their desk and everything is cluttered, making things hard to find. Do you really need the stress ball that you got from the trade show five years ago? So evaluate and eliminate any clutter that you have on top of your desk, and then do a review of each drawer of your desk and any other furniture such as bookshelves, filing cabinets, etc. One of the challenges of getting and staying organized is having too many things. One of the secrets of getting organized is to have fewer things to keep track of, file, and sort. If you haven't used it or tested it for over six months, unless it is important to keep for legal reasons (such as an important file), toss it, recycle it, or give it away. This includes getting rid of all the extra pens and pencils that have been sitting in a cup on your desk for the last decade, and there's only one kind you like to use anyway. It's funny—in our family I only like to use a certain kind of writing pen, and my husband only likes to use a certain kind of that as well, and we have decided that all the other pens just need to be tossed because they're never going to be used. They just sat there taking up space. It's just getting in the way of your progress and cluttering up your desk.

### Idea #4—Stuff needs a spot—have a spot to keep your "stuff"

Everyone at work comes into the office, and they have things that they need to put down. A woman will have a purse that she needs to put away somewhere, and perhaps a briefcase as well. A man will have a briefcase and perhaps some other item. So if you have car keys, every day after you arrive at your office where do you put your car keys or your employee badge (if you don't wear it around your neck on a lanyard) or your cell phone or your headset? The idea behind this concept is to have a place where stuff goes every time you come in. In our home, my husband has a little copper-colored box that sits inside the door in our house. When my husband comes home, he places his wallet, keys, cell phone, and headset all in the box. This simple technique will save you hours of time having to search for something that you don't remember where you left. Having a consistent spot for your stuff is extremely helpful.

### Idea #5—Traffic cop your desk

Come up with a traffic pattern for your desk—when you are at work, things arrive at your desk in physical form. It could be the mail, or an invoice for approval, or hundreds of other kinds of work-related documents that end up in something called your "in basket." Most people have an in basket, but here's the problem—on the desk they do not have a "how-to basket"; they have not made a determination as to the order in which things should go as they go through the process of being worked on. So, for example, suppose an invoice arrives in my basket for approval. Many people will take the invoice out of the basket, review it, sign off on it, and then lay it on their desk. They don't then immediately put that invoice into their out basket. So I just want you to analyze, when something comes across your desk, where it comes in, how it was worked on, and where it goes. Think of it as a production line in an automobile factory—the cars come in, and in each station something is added before they go out and leave the factory. What is the flow of paperwork from incoming to your desk to outgoing from your desk.

It is just a matter of what works best for you and figuring out when you are most productive. If you can figure that out, then it is like a car being in the right gear. In the right gear, you are more productive and efficient.

# WORK IT!

Are you a night owl or an early bird?

_____

_____

_____

How do you know that?

_____

_____

_____

In the past, have you arranged your time around when you are at your best?

_____

_____

_____

Do you consider other people's MPZs when you work with them?

_____

_____

_____

In terms of space, where are you at your most productive?

_____

_____

_____

_____

_____

In terms of space, where are you at your least productive? Why?

_____

_____

_____

_____

What do you need to change about your desk area in order to be more productive?

_____

_____

_____

_____

How would that help?

_____

_____

_____

_____

## CHAPTER SIX

### JOLT #6
# MAKE AND KEEP A TO-DO LIST

## THE POWER OF THE TO-DO LIST

*"I'm a big believer in to-do lists. I think of five things in the shower. I set goals and get my work done, but I have to plan for fun things, too. I'm always thinking about what will make my family happier. So I set up playdates and trips."*
—HEIDI KLUM

In this chapter, I would like to talk about one of the most important and essential tools for being productive, and that is the to-do list. As I mentioned in another chapter, it is important to have specific goals personally and professionally, and then to plan exactly how you're going to achieve those goals. Once you have your goals and your plans for the year, and then for the quarter, the month, and the week, then, of course, you will have the things you need to do every day. The tool that you will use to do this is the world famous to-do list. I have met many very successful people, and all of them seem to have one thing in common—they have goals, and they definitely do have an active daily to-do list.

Let me give you some tools and techniques that I think you will find very helpful in order to use a to-do list effectively.

## THE LIST SHOULD BE ALIGNED WITH YOUR GOALS

Obviously, every day you're going to write out a to-do list, and it should be aligned with your annual, quarterly, monthly, and weekly goals. There will, of course, be other items on the list that are not necessarily directly aligned with your goals that you definitely need to get done that particular week or day. The problem that I see often is people have very specific goals, but when I review the daily to-do list, there are no activities or tasks that are aligned with the goals, so I see they never get anything achieved relating to them.

## THE LIST SHOULD BE IN WRITING

I do not know any successful people who have their to-do list in their head; they always seem to have them in writing. You may write your to-do list on your phone, on a legal pad, in a composition book, on a plain piece of white paper, in your calendar, or use your laptop, or you may choose from many other ways of recording your to-do list electronically or manually. It doesn't matter what format it takes; I just want you to make sure that you have all of your items listed on your to-do list for that day in writing. Having your to-do items in writing helps you to do several things: 1) it keeps you on track with exactly what you need to do; 2) obviously, it helps you keep track of what you've already done; 3) you can add to the list whenever something new comes up that particular day; 4) when someone asks you to do something, you can compare what you need to do for someone versus what you have on your list; 5) I think it gives you more credibility; and 6) it makes you more effective and productive because you're never in doubt as to what it is you have to do.

## THERE SHOULD BE CATEGORIES

I believe in order to have an effective to-do list, a good idea is to think about categories on the list. For example, on my daily to-do list, I will often have the following categories:

- Tasks to complete
- Administrative work
- E-mail
- Phone calls
- Travel arrangements
- Meetings
- Preparations
- Household
- Financial
- Social

These are obviously just suggestions, but the idea of having categories on your to-do list is to be able to divide them up into logical segments. An additional advantage I see in having a categorized to-do list is that if I have seven phone calls to make and have them listed, then when I make those calls I have them in the right category; I don't have them spread around over different places on the list.

## PRIORITIZATION

Obviously, any time someone prepares a to-do list for the day, there are going to be some things that are more important than others. Some items may have more weight and more urgency and more importance. Many experts who have talked about time and about getting things done have used different ways of describing how to prioritize items on the to-do list. In his book, Alan Lakein described categorizing items for your to-do list as items prioritized as A, B, or C. He then even suggested assigning priorities to each category so that there could be an A-1, A-2, or A-3. Dr. Stephen Covey, the author of *The 7 Habits of Highly Effective People,* referred to looking at items on a to-do list and identifying the things that were the "big rocks," another way of describing what was important. He also talked about having items in categories. There were some items that were important and urgent, and some items that were not urgent but important; you should make room to do both of those in your to-do list. I believe that no matter what approach you take, you are going to have to define which items are most important and which ones you should do in which order. Whether these have numbers or letters or stars or asterisks is completely up to you.

## A TO-DO LIST IS A CONTINUOUS TOOL

It seems funny to say that a daily to-do list is a continuous tool, because the name itself would imply that it's only done daily. Here are a few things to think about. I may start out at the beginning of the week on Monday having a very defined list of things I need to do on Monday. However, life at work can get interesting because it is a fast-paced world. Despite your very clean and neat and efficient to-do list for the day, you often will get thrown curveballs by people that you work with, including your boss. You may not actually be able to complete everything that's on your to-do list, and you also may have things added to your to-do list for various reasons. A to-do list becomes a written living document that is constantly changing and flexing depending on what you're doing that particular day and how much time you have available. My recommendation is that if you do have a daily to-do list, anything you do that does not get done should be immediately transferred to the following list for the next day.

## MARK AS YOU GO

When you are working with a daily to-do list, you need to come up with some type of system that helps you mark which tasks have been completed and which ones still remain. What I find interesting is my wife and I both use somewhat different systems in terms of marking items off our lists. I use a certain color of highlighter to highlight items that have been completed, and my wife marks the items off with a pen. There are no right answers; you just have to experiment to figure out what works for you.

## INCLUDE TIME ESTIMATES

When you take the time to write out your daily to-do list, you may also want to include a rough estimates of how long that item is going to take. This will help you to determine whether your estimation was accurate or not and will give you a much better idea of how long things take in the future. I think it also tells you whether you are being realistic if you put down 30 items that need an hour to get done, because you are probably not going to get all those things done in one day.

## HAVING A TO-DO LIST MAKES YOU MORE CREDIBLE

How does a to-do list make you more credible? Let's say that your manager walks into your office at the beginning of the day and asks you a question that almost every manager in the world would ask—"so what are you working on today?" If you're a highly intelligent, well-prepared individual, you will then reach over and grab your to-do list and read off all the items you are working on for the day and for the week. Because many people do not do this, you certainly will make a favorable impression and increase your credibility with anyone who asks what it is that you're working on.

## A TO-DO LIST INCREASES FOCUS

It is so easy to get caught up in the noise and the busyness of the workday that it's sometimes easy to forget what it is you're supposed to be working on. To me, a to-do list is kind of your map for the day, which you can always refer to throughout the day to remind yourself of what it is you had planned to work on. Let's say, for example, you get called into an unscheduled meeting for two hours, which you obviously did not plan for. Once you're out of the meeting, you can go back to your desk and look over your list and remind yourself of what you're working on. This allows you to refocus your plan in accordance with your surprise schedule that you did not exactly plan for.

## INCLUDE WORK ITEMS AND OTHER PERSONAL ITEMS IN THE SAME LIST

I do not think that people can successfully live their life in isolation, and having a list of both personal and professional items is much more efficient and effective. Let's say that you are at work and you go on your lunch break (incidentally, I find that as I travel all over the country, unfortunately, many people now are not even taking a lunch break). Then on your lunch break you can look at your to-do list to determine if there are personal items that you can work on as you are eating your lunch.

## HAVE YOUR TO-DO LIST WITH YOU AT ALL TIMES

As you do your work throughout the day, I strongly suggest having your to-do list with you wherever it is that you go. If you have to run errands, you should take your to-do list with you; if you're in a meeting, you should bring your to-do list with you; if you're on the road traveling for business, your list should be with you as well. So the reality is that no matter where you are, your to-do list should accompany you wherever you go to help inform you of what it is that you're supposed to be working on at any time. Believe me, if you do not have your to-do list with you, you'll find that you need to refer to it and because you don't have it, that will be frustrating.

## REVIEW YOUR LIST FREQUENTLY THROUGHOUT THE DAY

I have often seen people who at the beginning of the day will write out a to-do list, but then they do not refer to the list as they get so caught up in their day-to-day work. Then at the end of the day they look at their to-do list and realize there were many things in it that they forgot to do because they were so caught up in everything else. Throughout the day, when you have a quick moment, you should pick up your to-do list and review it to keep yourself on track, and to track and mark off items that you have completed.

## A TO-DO LIST CAN BE VERY MOTIVATING

When you have a long list of things to be done, and are able to start checking them off the list, it can give you a tremendous feeling of accomplishment. If you work for a company, you can also save these to-do lists, and it will help you when you have your annual performance reviews because you will have a list of all of the things that you have accomplished, in some sort of organized time frame. We often do so much at work we actually forget exactly what we achieved, and when we have our performance review meeting, we forget what we did throughout the year. The daily to-do list will help you remember what it is that you forgot to do.

## A TO-DO LIST WILL HELP YOU KEEP YOUR PROMISES

I have worked in many organizations throughout my career and have talked to someone and asked them for information, resources, or to work on a specific small piece of a project. Unfortunately, those folks often promised that they would do what they said they would do, but later did not produce the results. When I contacted them to remind them about what they had promised to do, unfortunately the answer would often be that they got busy and just forgot. Without meaning to be too blunt, I must be honest and say that "I forgot" is really not a very credible excuse for the world of business. Yes, people can be delayed, and people can have problems, challenges, and issues. But telling a coworker or your boss that you did not complete a project will certainly damage your credibility. As simplistic as it may be, a to-do list is a great tool to help you ensure that you don't forget to do something for someone.

## A TO-DO LIST WILL HELP CLARIFY YOUR THINKING

Even though a to-do list is a somewhat simplistic tool, and it is not a particular form of genius, it helps you think through what it is that you need to work on and what exactly you need to accomplish. I teach creativity and innovation, and one concept I talk about in creativity and innovation training is that of displayed thinking. Research indicates that writing ideas down helps to increase our creativity; it helps to stimulate clearer and better thinking. So believe it or not, writing down your to-do list will help clarify your thinking and probably will help enhance your level of creativity as well.

## DEADLINES

When you write out your to-do list, make sure to also include any deadlines that may be important on the list. Often in the world of business an item that needs to be done is tied to a specific deadline, and if the deadline is not met there may be some potentially serious consequences. On your to-do list you may have a lot of items that need to be done but are not quite as urgent. You also have other items that are extremely urgent and are tied to a very tight deadline. So knowing what the deadlines are also helps you evaluate how important each item is on the to-do list.

## MAKE SURE TO INCLUDE SUBTASKS

If I am working on a project and I write in my to-do list "work on the Wilson proposal," I may need to also include several subtasks that are related to achieving the larger one. For example, I may have different activities such as research, writing, e-mailing, and having meetings with certain people that would all involve working on the proposal itself. So the more specific you can make your to-do list and the more careful you are to include the subtasks, the more successful you will be in terms of productivity.

## MAKE SURE YOU CAN READ IT

At certain points in my life I have worked with people who have had to-do lists that they have scratched out on a piece of paper in order to plan their daily tasks. What is hilarious is when they pull up the list to refer to it, they can't read their own writing and they don't know what it says. If you have terrible handwriting, which is very difficult to read even for yourself, you may want to consider typing your list out and printing it from your computer.

## THE TIMING OF YOUR TO-DO LIST

One of the interesting elements of creating a to-do list is when you actually create it. As I travel around the country training and consulting people on time management and productivity, they often ask when they should do their to-do list.

My answer is actually "in three layers":

I believe that you should do your to-do list at the beginning of the week. So if my work week begins on Monday morning, it would probably be a great idea to plan on Sunday night my to-do list for the week.

This is a great advantage when I get up on Monday morning and go to work because I'm already locked and loaded and know exactly what I'm going to work on as soon as I walk in the door. Some people say they would rather go to the office first and create their to-do list when they get to the office. I don't think this is nearly as effective, but it is up to you to learn what works best for you. One reason I don't think this is as effective is oftentimes when people get to work intending to create their to-do list, they get caught up in the work so quickly that they never get to the to-do list because of time constraints. The second aspect of a to-do list is it is a continual process so you're going to be adding things to the list and deleting things from it throughout the day. The third aspect of the list is that you need to review your list at the end of the day to evaluate what is done and what still needs to be done the next day. Those items will then, of course, be carried over to the next day's to-do list.

## THE QUESTION ABOUT QUANTITY

There seems to be a great deal of debate about how many things should go on a daily to-do list. For example, if I spend eight hours at work, does it make sense to put 60 items on my to-do list when I'm never going to get all of them done? Some people say yes because putting them on the list just keeps you aware of them, and the items you don't get done today simply get moved to the next list. Other people say, "What is the point of putting a ton of things on the list, because they are not going to get done, so you would be much better off just saving those items to put on the next day's list." It really is completely up to you because one size does not fit all, and as soon as I would say what works for one person, I would have to say something else works for someone else. I also do believe that personality and preference play a part in the style of to-do list you want to use. To me, all that matters is the fact that you have one, that you use it, and and that you use it systematically.

I think a to-do list can be amazingly motivating. As Steve Maraboli once said:

> "Rename your 'To-Do' list to your 'Opportunities' list. Each day is a treasure chest filled with limitless opportunities; take joy in checking many off your list."

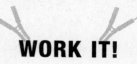

# WORK IT!

Do you use a daily to-do list?

_____

_____

_____

_____

If you don't, why not?

_____

_____

_____

_____

How would having a to-do list help you?

_____

_____

_____

_____

Do you prioritize your list?

_____

_____

_____

_____

What could you do to make your list more effective?

_____

_____

_____

_____

Is your list aligned with your goals?

_____

_____

_____

_____

# CHAPTER SEVEN

## *JOLT #7*
# STOP SAYING YES TO EVERYTHING AND START SAYING NO

## HOW TO SAY NO TO INCREASE PRODUCTIVITY

> *"Let today mark a new beginning for you. Give yourself permission to say NO without feeling guilty, mean, or selfish. Anybody who gets upset and/or expects you to say YES all of the time clearly doesn't have your best interest at heart. Always remember: You have a right to say NO without having to explain yourself. Be at peace with your decisions."*
> —STEPHANIE LAHART

In this chapter, I would like to talk about a very important concept that many people do not believe is related to productivity, but I believe that it is directly related to the lack of productivity— and that is the ability to say no. I meet many people who tell me that they're completely overwhelmed, and one of the reasons, they explain, is they really don't feel like they can say no! At work, in addition to the regular job responsibilities, they have volunteered for every committee and every subcommittee in the company. At home, they have volunteered to work in various functions at the children's schools and churches in their community. If someone asked them to do something socially, they almost always say yes, or they have a real conflict. The result is they are completely overwhelmed personally and professionally.

If your motivation for reading this book about productivity is to truly become more productive, then this is one chapter you really need to think about. If it is your habit and your approach to say yes to everything, that definitely has a big negative impact on your productivity.

## WHY WE SAY YES

Why do many people in life personally and professionally say yes when they really would rather say no? There are some very specific reasons I'd like you to think about and know if they apply to you and to think about if you do them.

### Politeness

I think most people want to feel like they are polite, and they make every attempt to try to get along with everyone. Most people were raised to say "please" and "thank you" and to be polite to everyone. Don't get me wrong—I think that politeness is a very good quality and makes our society a better place when we all treat each other with respect and kindness. The problem is when we take that concept and apply it to having the ability to say no. Someone asks you if you would like to attend the black tie affair for a charity that is coming up at the end of the month. For one reason or another you really do not feel like going, but instead of politely declining, you say "yes" when you really meant to say "no." Many people say, "Well, what is the big deal?" In terms of productivity, it actually is a big deal. You are going to be spending time and effort and energy not only in preparing to go to the event, but also in spending time at the event, and also shopping for a new outfit because it is a black tie event. While it may only seem like two hours of obligation, it is probably more like six or seven. The irony is all that time invested in something that you really did not want to do in the first place.

### You feel obligated

One of the reasons that people say yes when they really want to say no is they have a sense of obligation to the person who is asking. The person may be a family member, and they do not want to offend them by saying no. It may be someone at work who has done you a favor in the past, so you feel obliged to return the favor. I used to work for a company in the training department, and my boss used to like to have team building events. There was a team-building event that he would have once a quarter, when everyone would get together on a Saturday and go out on his boat. When the boss mentioned when the Saturday team building event was going to be, everyone on the team felt obligated to go, and that meant that they were sacrificing a large part of their Saturday. By the way, the boss also expected the *spouses* of those people to attend as well. So every quarter, the entire team went out on the boat, and it became extremely boring because we did the same activity, the same trip, the same routine every time. Everybody was doing it, not because they felt like doing it or because they enjoyed it, but because they felt obligated. Once, a team member informed my boss he was not going to be able to attend because he had a conflict that day. The boss met with him and told him that he was extremely disappointed and that he was "not being a good team member." I cite this instance because sometimes obligation is something that we just feel is true, and sometimes obligation is real and may have some negative consequences if we cannot meet our obligations, particularly if it relates to work. In the past, I have worked for companies that have had holiday parties, and it was well known that it was a *bad career move* not to show up. So it is up to you to decide whether the obligations are true or not, but my point is that in many cases people feel obligated when they really aren't obligated and it is just simply a choice.

### Fear

Often when people say yes, the main reason for their doing so is they are afraid of the consequences of saying no. When I ask people why they do this, they say it is because they're afraid that if they say no they're going to hurt someone else's feelings socially and professionally. They're also afraid of the person's potential reaction. For example, in a family, if grandmother is having her 90th birthday party in a faraway state, all the people in the family decide to go. If someone has a conflict or some other reason why they do not want to attend grandmother's birthday party, they are afraid to tell family members that they won't be attending because they think they will be upset or are afraid they will get into an argument. I have often heard fear described as *future events appearing real*, which I think is a good definition. In many cases, people fear the reaction of the person that they're going to be talking to and anticipate massive conflict, but find that after the discussion is done there was no conflict. Often, we overestimate the amount of conflict that is going to happen. Guess what?

It is our life, and we are not required to do anything unless we want to do it, except for paying taxes and dying. So if you want to get more control over your life and over your productivity, you just have to accept the fact that every now and then you are going to tell people no. I think way too many people are overly concerned about what other people think and how other people will react. Don't let this factor influence your decisions too greatly.

### Change your thinking about saying no

Many times I hear people say, "I am really bad at saying no." Or "I just can't help myself—I can't tell anyone no because if I do I feel really bad." Here is something that I definitely want you to think about—and it is the concept of self-talk. As a motivational speaker and book author, I often teach people how to adjust their self-talk to help them adjust their thinking. Unfortunately, if you keep saying something to yourself over and over again you'll believe it and it begins to become part of how you operate on a regular basis. So if I say to myself, "I just can't help myself; I can't say no," that's exactly what happens! What I want you to do is change your thinking and your language and say, "I am an intelligent adult—I do have the ability to make decisions, and sometimes I will say no and sometimes I will say yes." So being aware of what you say to yourself on a regular basis and trying to change what you say to yourself will definitely change your behavior.

### Suffering from the should

What do I mean when I say that people are suffering from the should? What I mean by that is often people do something because they believe that they *should* do it. I hear people say all the time, "I am going to go to that event because people told me that I should go." If we look up the word "should," does it sound a lot like the word "obligation"? I could use the same sentence and say, "I probably should go to that event because people are telling me that I'm obligated to go." Just because other people say that you *should* do something, it does not mean you have to do it.

### Feeling guilty

Often I hear people say that the reason why they do something is that they would feel guilty if they did not do it. When I ask them why they would feel guilty about not doing it, they give me a whole host of reasons as to why they should. None of them are very logical. They may say, "Because I always go every year" or "If I don't go I'll feel bad about it" or "I really need to go do my part." You get the idea—people come up with all sorts of reasons for feeling guilty. The hardcore reality of the situation is that in many cases the guilt has absolutely no basis in reality whatsoever. The only reason I think you should feel guilty is if you deliberately do something to hurt someone or if you're being mean, hateful, or spiteful. If you're not doing any of those things, you should release the idea of feeling guilty.

### Reciprocation

Sometimes I hear people say that they said yes when they meant no because they *have to* reciprocate a good turn the other person had previously done. They will say, "Well, I have to go to their event this year because two years ago they came to mine." Or they will say, "I need to do this person a favor, as they have done many favors for me." So does this mean that if someone does you a favor, you always have to pay it back, or if someone does A for me, I have to do B for them? This is the tit for tat formula—you have to see that in most cases the other person is not keeping track of the numbers and is not necessarily expecting you to reciprocate. We, in our minds, think that they are keeping track when the reality is they are not. If you've done someone a lot of favors and they have done you a lot of favors, don't worry about direct one-to-one reciprocation.

## WHY WE SHOULD SAY NO

In terms of productivity, there actually are some very powerful reasons why we should learn to say no.

### Productivity

You have heard the saying, "you only have so many hours in the day." There are only so many hours in the day, and there are only so many hours in the week, in the month, and in the year. One of the ways of increasing your productivity is to make sure you maximize your time. When you have a hard time saying no, you then take away from your productivity time—you've obligated yourself to spend time in some other way. By saying no, you can dramatically enhance your productivity.

### Distraction

When you have a hard time saying no and you obligate yourself to doing things you don't want to do, it not only takes your time, your effort, your labor, and your energy, it also takes away what I call "mind share." To use an analogy, let's say your mind is like the stock market and has 1000 shares available in order to be productive. You obligate yourself to other activities and let's say that activity cost you 100 shares in terms of time. I would passionately argue that it's taking not only 100 shares in terms of time but also perhaps another 100 shares in terms of distraction. The amount of time, effort, and energy, and labor you put into thinking about that particular activity also costs you in terms of productivity; you could be thinking about something else that was more productive.

### Cost

You have a hard time saying no, and you obligate yourself to doing something that is going to cost you in some way, shape, or form. It may cost, time, effort, and labor. It may also cost you in terms of real dollars. If your boss invites you to attend his daughter's wedding, that's obviously going to cost you because you're going to need to buy a gift for the daughter, then you are going to be investing in gas to get to the event, and if the event is out of town, you will also be incurring travel expenses. Many times when we say yes to something, we do not realize how much it will cost us in terms of real dollars.

## HOW TO DECIDE IF YOU'RE GOING TO SAY YES OR NO

Many people tell me that when they get a request, they have a hard time deciding whether to do it or not and don't really know how to decide. Here are some tips to help you decide whether to say yes or no.

### Ask yourself the first major question

The first major question should really be whether you feel like doing it or not. After all, if you want to and you are available, there really are no other questions—go and enjoy it.

### Is this aligned with my goals?

When you're trying to decide whether to do something or not, whether to say yes or no, you may want to refer to your written goals that were addressed in an earlier chapter. Then just simply ask yourself, is this aligned with my goals either directly or indirectly?

### Will this result in conflict?

In trying to decide whether to say yes or no, is there going to be conflict created if I say no? Is there going to be conflict that will be a result of saying yes? If there is a conflict, will the conflict be long term or short term, and if there is a conflict, am I willing to live with the consequences of the conflict?

### What will be the impact?

When determining whether to say yes or no, what will be the overall impact for you if you say yes? What will be the overall impact on them if you say no? What will be the impact on you professionally? What would be the impact on you personally?

### How will this affect other people?

When evaluating whether you say yes or no, you may also want to evaluate the potential impact it will have on other people. The result of your decision may have a positive or a negative impact, but it is a good idea to think that through before you decide.

One other note—make sure that you're not intimidated or bullied by people who want to try to manipulate you into doing something. As an adult you need to develop a spine and be willing to stand up to people who try to manipulate you by using guilt or anger or hostility to get you to do something. As Rosie Blyth once said, "Whether they're family or friends, manipulators are difficult to escape from. Give in to their demands and they'll be happy enough, but if you develop a spine and start saying no, it will inevitably bring a fresh round of head games and emotional blackmail. You'll notice that breaking free from someone else's dominance will often result in them accusing you of being selfish. Yes, you're selfish, because you've stopped doing what they want you to do for them. Wow. Can these people hear themselves?!"

## THINK ABOUT NEGOTIATING

When it comes to saying yes or no, also think about this—it is possible to negotiate with the person who is asking. For example, if my company is heavily involved in some sort of initiative for charity and they want me to participate in being part of a planning committee, I could say:

"I can't be on the committee, but I would be happy to donate some money to the cause."

"I can't be on the committee, but I would be happy to help out and volunteer to do something else."

"I can't be on the committee, but I would like to volunteer my efforts on the graphics."

So the idea behind negotiating is that when you tell someone no, give them some options about what you could do if you want to make that offer. Keep in mind, however, that it still is okay to say no and not come back with a counteroffer.

## COMMUNICATION

People who have a hard time saying no also have a very hard time communicating with the person who is asking, particularly if they're going to say no. They are uncomfortable and awkward and don't really know how to go about saying it. Here are some suggestions about communicating when you're going to say no.

### Thank them

Whenever anyone asks you to do something, it is a good idea to start out declining by saying, "Thank you very much for your offer, I appreciate you thinking of me."

### Decline directly

Say to the person who asked you, "I really appreciate you asking me that, but, unfortunately, I'm not able to make it because I have a conflict." If you feel comfortable saying it, you can say, "Maybe I can attend sometime in the future."

### Don't explain your conflict

You are not obligated to tell the other person what your conflict is. In other words, if you say, "I appreciate you asking me; I'm, unfortunately, not able to attend because I have a conflict." You don't have to say you're going to grandmother's 95th birthday party. In fact, you do not have to explain at all.

### Don't be negative or overly apologetic

I believe that when you tell someone no, you should keep it short and sweet. Don't say to the other person, "Boy, I sure feel like a total loser—I am so sorry that I have to tell you that I can't attend." This negative apologetic approach is one I really do believe damages credibility. Just decline in a nice friendly manner, which shows grace and poise.

### Decide on your communication channel

Depending on the context of the situation, you need to decide if you're going to decline the person's offer verbally in person, verbally by phone, by e-mail if it's at work, or with a handwritten note. Whichever form you choose, make sure that you communicate with the person sooner rather than later, but make sure to do it in a very pleasant and friendly manner. I do believe that, obviously, the most effective form of communication is talking to the person directly, or if you're in a different area of the country, then talking to the person by phone. The least effective form of communication, of course, is e-mail, because to me e-mail is the least effective way of conveying your real meaning, and it is very open to misinterpretation.

So decide you are going to say no when you mean no and yes when you mean yes.

> *"Until you learn how to confidently say NO to so many things, you shall always say YES to so many things. The real summary of a regretful life is a life that failed to balance YES and NO. Yes! A life that failed to recognize when to courageously say NO and when to confidently say YES!"*
> —ERNEST AGYEMANG YEBOAH

# WORK IT!

Do you have a hard time saying no?

_____

_____

_____

_____

Is it more in your professional life or personal life?

_____

_____

_____

_____

Why are you hesitant about saying no?

_____

_____

_____

_____

When do you need to say _no_ more? How would that help you?

_____

_____

_____

_____

What technique for saying no did you like best?

_____

_____

# CHAPTER EIGHT

## JOLT #8
# CONTROL THE INTERRUPTIONS

## PARDON THE INTERRUPTIONS: HOW TO CONTROL THEM

*"Being constantly the hub of a network of potential interruptions provides the excitement and importance of crisis management. As well as the false sense of efficiency in multitasking, there is the false sense of urgency in multi-interrupt processing."*
—MICHAEL FOLEY

In this chapter, we're going to talk about one of the most insidious drains on productivity, and that is interruption. It seems like at work we are constantly getting interrupted multiple times per day, maybe even multiple times each hour. That makes it very difficult to focus and also difficult to be productive. I talk to many people who start work at the beginning of the day with a list of things they need to get done, and at the end of the day nothing on the list is done because everything they did that day was interrupted by someone else.

So how do we solve this dilemma? We solve the dilemma by working to try as much as possible to gain control over the interruptions.

I know that there are several factors that contribute to more interruptions in today's workplace:

### Technology

Because of technology, people unrealistically expect that they will be able to reach you at any time of the day. They can call you on the phone, they can e-mail you, they can text you, they can instant message you, and in many corporate cultures people expect you to answer no matter when they contact you. This is an unrealistic expectation that people have, which leads to constant interruption of your day.

### Open floor space

The offices of today are now being designed with what they call the "open office environment" where there are no offices, no walls, and no cubes. This, in my opinion, leads to constant distraction, constant interruption, and the constant wall of noise that people are subjected to throughout the day.

### Multitasking

I was facilitating a leadership program last week, and one of the participants in the program said that at any point during the day she was on e-mail and the phone at the same time and at most times also had somebody standing at her desk waiting to ask her a question. She smiled and said, "Just so you understand that's how it is all day long, and it never changes."

So what can we do about? Let me give you some suggestions:

## IN-PERSON INTERRUPTIONS

An in-person interruption is when you're sitting in your workspace and someone comes to ask you a question who does not have an appointment and arrives unannounced. This person often will say, "Do you have a minute?" but the irony is that the person never takes a minute, but takes multiple minutes after he or she starts talking. What do we do in that situation? I actually think there are several things that we can do in order to be proactive and in order to increase our productivity:

### *Try to negotiate with that person*

Say, "I am terribly sorry, I'm currently in the middle of working on something and could get back with you in about _____" (and fill in the time request). In many cases this forces the person to realize that they are interrupting you, and they will agree to come back at the time that you agree to, which will be later on. This ends up taking an interruption and making it into an appointment. I'm not saying that this technique always works; sometimes, people do have something that is urgent and need an answer immediately, but in many cases if you ask them to wait between 30 minutes and an hour they are willing to come back. If the person is paying a social call to tell you about something that happened on the weekend, then use more or less the same technique. Say to them, "That sounds like an incredible story, and I'd love to hear everything that happened; can you and I catch up later on so I can hear all the details?" This tells the person that you still care about what they have to say, but also signals to them in a nice way that you're in the middle of something and will have to hear their story later on.

### Try putting on a set of earbuds

This is a psychological ploy, but one that is often very effective. If you're sitting at your desk working on something and you have earbuds in your ears, people are much less likely to come up and interrupt you. By the way, it doesn't matter if you have music playing or not; it just matters that they are visible to the person who's thinking about interrupting you.

### Try the technique of isolation

People can't interrupt you if they cannot find you. So one strategy you may want to think about is moving to a conference room, an empty office, or an open corner, but somewhere in your office space where people actually cannot see you. The advantage of this is you will have a lot fewer interruptions because people can't interrupt you if they can't find you. I call this the "hide and seek" technique, and it is very effective. Another approach you may want to try (which is subject to your boss's approval) is to ask to work from home if you are working on a complex project that requires a lot of concentration. If you are not physically present in the office, the only way people can interrupt you is through other technology, not in person.

### Don't make eye contact

When you are working on a project in the office, particularly in an open office environment, try to stay focused on what you're working on and try not to look up at others. For some reason, when you look up at others they assume you're not working on something, and they will then come over and interrupt what you are doing.

### Come up with some team guidelines

If you are on a team of several people, have a meeting and talk about what should be the guidelines relating to interrupting each other. I work with organizations that have offices, and they come up with an agreement that when their door is open, people can come in and interrupt; when the door is cracked, they can come in only if it's important; and when the door is closed, they may not interrupt the person at all. For people who work in cubes, they end up using three pieces of paper (red, yellow, and green), which have the same meanings as a door being opened, cracked, or closed. In an open office environment, you certainly can do the same color coding by putting a folding table tent a certain color beside you to indicate your availability. You probably also need to discuss the times or the situations when it's okay to interrupt someone else and when it's not. The bottom line is if the team can get together and mutually agree on how you're all going to handle interruptions, you probably will get more done as a team overall. The challenge most times to teams is they never talk about how they're going to be interrupting each other, and that becomes the problem.

## PHONE INTERRUPTIONS

I do find it amusing that when the phone rings most people feel compelled to answer immediately no matter what they are in the middle of doing. Obviously, if you're in customer service you would be obligated to answer the phone when it rings because that's your job. But if you have some other function at work, it does not necessarily mean that you have to answer the phone immediately. If you're in the middle of a project you certainly can have the call go to voice mail and call that person back a little bit later when you are done with your project or are at a good stopping point. The second technique people often use is they will answer the phone and say to the person on the other end, "Hello Walter, I appreciate your calling; I am in the middle of something right now, could call you back—say in an hour?" Now, obviously, you're interrupting what you are doing to answer the phone and tell the person you are not available, but sometimes this makes the person on the other end feel a little more valued because you acknowledged their call and told them that you will call back later. I do believe that we have reached a phase in our world where people are getting spoiled by technology and have little to no patience. The impact this has on phone calls is that when someone calls you, they almost expect you to call them back right away. This is an unrealistic but common demand these days, and people do expect an immediate response. If you answer the phone all day long, you certainly will not be productive, and the only time you'll be able to do work is either before eight o'clock in the morning or after five o'clock at night. On a personal level, this also applies to your cell phone. Just because your cell phone rings in the middle of dinner it does not mean that you have to answer it. Yet I see people all over the country who are answering the phone in the middle of meals in restaurants, in the middle of a date, on a plane right before it takes off. There do not seem to be any limits as to when the phone is being answered. I was recently in an airport restroom where a man actually answered his phone in the restroom! Really? Cell phones also have voice mail.

## E-MAIL INTERRUPTIONS

How can e-mail be an interruption? I find that many people at work find e-mail to be a massive interruption because people that they work with are often expecting an immediate response to an e-mail they just sent. Additionally, many people set up their preferences on their computer to hear a tone whenever a new e-mail comes in. So someone can be in the middle of an important project, but because they hear that *ding* sound they will immediately stop what they're doing and check their e-mail. This then becomes an interruption, which is actually worse than personal interruption because it happens more frequently throughout the day. What happens is a person is working on a project, then checking e-mails, then working on a project, then checking e-mails; in other words, they are bouncing back and forth between those two things. So here are a few suggestions about handling e-mail/text/IM interruptions:

### You do not have to respond immediately

Try to block out several times a day when you're just answering e-mail instead of answering it all day long.

### Turn off your notification sound

That tells you that you just received an e-mail—that way you will not be as tempted to check it when you hear that tone.

### Avoid the temptation

When you are in the middle of doing something, avoid the temptation of stopping that and checking e-mail, because it will immediately distract you from whatever you're doing.

If anyone sends you an e-mail and they criticize you for not responding, simply tell them you are sorry but you are in the middle of a critically important project, which was urgent.

## MEETING INTERUPTIONS

Meetings can certainly also be a form of interruption even though they are often scheduled in your calendar system. If you start out the day working on a particular initiative and then several times a day have to stop what you're doing to attend various meetings, then those are obviously an interruption to your day. When I was a vice president in corporate America, I often attended meetings throughout the day from anywhere between seven o'clock in the morning to six o'clock at night. What I discovered by going to various meetings is that each time I went back to my office, it would be hard for me to get into the flow and get back into focusing on whatever I was working on before I left. So meetings can definitely be a drain on your productivity. So what can you do to make meetings less of a drain on your productivity? If you have any control over the meeting whatsoever, here are a few things that you can do:

### Have an agenda

I find that meetings are much more productive and successful when we have a specific and clear agenda for running the meeting.

### There needs to be a facilitator

I often see meetings that are chaotic and unorganized, and one of the reasons that they are that way is there is no one actually running the meeting.

### Know the objective

I often see meetings that people have, and I do not think that they have a very clear objective as to what they want to try to achieve in the meeting.

### Decide whether you should attend

One of the trends right now that I see in corporate America that I find interesting is that people have access to everyone's calendar: Instead of people scheduling themselves to go to a meeting, they get scheduled. I often talk to people who say they go to a meeting and have no earthly idea why it is that they are there. If you want to be productive, one of the things that you can do is to contact the person who scheduled you for the meeting and determine from them why it is that you need to be there. Sometimes people just invite everyone in kind of a carte blanche approach, and when you talk to them they say, "I don't really think you need to be there; I just wanted to invite you as a courtesy." If you can negotiate not being in meetings, it could massively impact your productivity every week by eliminating meeting time for meetings you really don't need to be at anyway.

Those are some things to think about in terms of controlling interruptions throughout the day. It's entirely up to you to decide how proactive you're going to be controlling interruptions, but I guarantee you that if you can try to control them, it will massively improve your level of productivity on a daily basis.

> *"It takes 25 minutes to recover from a phone call or an e-mail, researchers have found, and yet the average person receives such an interruption every 11 minutes. Which means that we're never caught up; we're always out of breath, running behind."*
> —Pico Iyer

# WORK IT!

Do you get interrupted often?

_____

_____

_____

_____

What are the main sources of interruption at work?

_____

_____

_____

_____

Which ones do you have some control over?

_____

_____

_____

_____

Do you negotiate when people come by unannounced?

_____

_____

_____

_____

What are some of the techniques that would work best for you for controlling interruptions?

_____

_____

_____

_____

How will this help you?

_____

_____

_____

_____

# CHAPTER NINE

## JOLT #9
# USE TECHNOLOGY TO BE MORE PRODUCTIVE

## I HAVE A ROBOT: USING TECHNOLOGY TO GET MORE DONE NOW

*"The first rule of any technology used in a business is that automation applied to an efficient operation will magnify the efficiency. The second is that automation applied to an inefficient operation will magnify the inefficiency."*
—BILL GATES

When I was a kid in elementary school, I remember watching documentaries about the future of technology, and I remember in almost every one of them they would say, "In the future, technology will help people increase efficiency at work, which means they will only have to work 30 hours a week and will have much more free time with their families." When we look back at it now, it almost seems laughable—technology has increased exponentially since I was a kid, but still it seems as if people are working longer hours and working harder despite the assistance from technology.

That said, I think technology can be a huge boost for your productivity and can help you work smarter and become much more productive. So the question is, what can you do to be more productive using technology that is all around you, available, and in many cases very inexpensive?

Before we get into a discussion of using technology to increase your productivity, I think there are some elements that you need to consider that may be downsides to technology before you make the leap.

### Technology can be a drain

What I mean by that is that if technology becomes too complex or too hard to operate, then the technology, instead of making someone more productive, actually makes them counterproductive; and then it is an actual drain on productivity, not an enhancement.

### Technology can be bright and shiny

I think sometimes people use technology just because it is cool or hip or edgy, not because it is necessarily the best use of a person's time and energy. Let's say I decide I'm going to switch to an online cloud-based technology for my time management, when before that I used a paper time management system that was incredibly effective and productive. So switching to technology just to switch does not really make a lot of sense, particularly if what you have is already working quite well.

### There can be breakdowns

Technology absolutely can be a wonderful tool for increasing productivity; however, I can't help it make me more productive if it doesn't work. So, for example, if you're using a cloud-based application to do something related to work and for some reason cannot get access to the Internet to access the cloud, then you have a problem. There can also be technical snafus for software that is not updating properly, or software on one side is not talking to software on the other. For example, I might use a time management system on my phone and enter a date into my system for an appointment. I can then log on later in the day to the same time management system and find that the appointment is not on my desktop calendar but only on my phone because the two devices were not talking to each other.

### Variation in platforms

If you have an organization in which some people are on one system (whatever the system may be) and other people are on a different system, there definitely will be a technological problem because different people are on different systems.

### Expense

While much technology is free or inexpensive, there are also some software packages or applications that actually charge a monthly or yearly fee, which can definitely add up.

So those are some elements of technology that I definitely want you to think about and consider as you use technology.

Here are some areas of technology that definitely may help you in terms of your productivity.

## E-MAIL

Here is an excerpt about e-mail from Rachael Doyle's book *Organize Your Business*:

> I think e-mail is the best thing that has ever happened to us and the worst thing that has ever happened to us. It's the best because we can communicate fast with

anyone in the world and send information anywhere and even include an attachment. It used to take us a long time to send information by mail, and it was very slow. It's the worst because it has often taken the place of communication that should be happening in person. It is also open to a lot of miscommunication. Different people perceive messages in different ways. Lastly, in many cases it has become a huge time drain (and brain drain), and it's very overwhelming to have an inbox with hundreds (or even thousands) of e-mails. My hope is I can give you some tools to help organize your e-mails and save you some time and energy.

### Idea #1—Don't worry, have a category

Take some time to sit down and think about on paper or electronically all of the categories you wish to have in your e-mail system folders. You may have different folders for some of the following categories: sales, marketing, financial, vendors, partners, projects, etc. Once you have your categories designated to have a file for each one, you then create subfolders under the name categories. For example, I can have a singular folder that is named "projects", but then I can have subfolders under that category that have individual product names for them.

### Idea #2—Keep, delete, or complete

Each time you have an e-mail that you have read or are processing there are three major decisions you need to make: Does this e-mail need to be deleted, kept in your inbox, or is it one that needs to be filed? If it needs to be deleted, then delete it immediately. If it needs to be filed, pick a category, as mentioned in idea number one, and immediately move the documents to that folder. That way you will always know where that particular e-mail is located. This will save you a lot of time and effort trying to locate a specific e-mail because you can just look at that respective folder.

### Idea #3—Color code to reduce the load

In some e-mail systems such as Outlook, you are able to color code the color of the e-mail depending on who the e-mail was from. For example, you can go in and under settings designate that all e-mails from your boss are going to be in red, all e-mails that are sent to you directly will be in blue, and all e-mails that are sent to you as CCs will be in purple. This gives you a color coding system. This way when you open up your e-mail inbox, you'll be able to quickly prioritize which e-mails you want to answer first, and quite frankly you may at times want to just delete the ones that are CCs—because the person did not send you an e-mail directly.

### Idea #4—Draw the line

One way of helping to keep your e-mails more organized is to make sure that your subject line is as specific as possible. For example, if you send someone an e-mail regarding the meeting in May, don't just use your subject line as "Meeting in May." On the subject line say something specific, like "Catering for meeting in May." One of the reasons you want to do this is there will be a time down the road when you are looking at 50 or 60 e-mails all relating to the meeting in May. If every subject line just says "meeting in May" you have to look at all of them. If a subject line reads "catering for meeting in

May," it will be much easier to find. Additionally when you're responding to someone else, don't keep their subject line; change it to one that you can keep track of.

### Idea #5—Cluttered inbox, cluttered mind

On a regular and consistent basis you should go to your e-mail and make sure to follow the three steps outlined in idea #2 (keep, delete, or complete). In addition to those steps, you should also take a look at all of the e-mails you get that are unsolicited that somehow over time you have started subscribing to. If you keep getting the same irrelevant e-mails (some would even call this spam) then take a few moments and unsubscribe to those e-mail sources; this will eliminate many items from your daily inbox volume.

### Idea #6—Now is the time

Far too often I see people go through a process which I find very interesting: they open an e-mail, take the time to read it, and then move on to another e-mail. The error they're making is they are not responding to that e-mail at the time; they are saving it to look at it at a later time. I'm not saying that they are not exceptions where an e-mail might be amazingly complicated and you will need to get to it later, but generally speaking, people will take the same e-mail and look at it and read it several times before taking any action. This is a waste of time and a redundant activity, so if you're going to read it, once you have read it then take the steps to complete it. Try to only "touch" each e-mail once. It is also much easier to take an e-mail and move it into a folder when your mind is fresh and you can remember what the e-mail was even about.

### *Idea #7—Consolidate to keep it straight*

Many people have various e-mail addresses, such as their e-mail at work, their e-mail at home, their e-mail for the charitable board that they serve on, or any combination thereof. Many have a list of several different e-mails that they need to check, if not each day, at least once a week. Using the services of a technical person, try to consolidate all of your e-mail accounts into one consistent source. This task can be done by having a forwarding program: take all e-mails from all accounts and forward them to one place; that way you only have one spot to check, and it's much more organized because it's in one place.

### *Idea #8—Negate notifications*

One of the interesting things I've noticed is that if you go on Facebook and make one comment on a friend's page about something they posted, then every time anyone else from the planet makes a comment to that same discussion thread, you end up getting an e-mail notification saying that "Billy Bob commented on your friend's posting." While this e-mail notification seems like a good idea in theory, in practice it ends up being a terrible interruption of your time throughout the day because you're inundated with e-mail notifications from any of your social media such as Facebook, LinkedIn, Pinterest, or Twitter. One thing that can save you a lot of time and energy and give you fewer e-mails to organize is to go into each of those social media platforms and turn off the notification buttons.

### Idea #9—Filter out the noise

Almost all e-mail systems have the ability to create filters. The idea behind filters is you can automatically set up those e-mails to go directly to a folder that is labeled for that particular topic. This way they will not distract you while you are working; you can look at them when you choose to look at them, not when the system sent you them. So find out from your IT department or look up online how to set up filters in your respective e-mail program.

### Idea #10—E-mail fail

Decide when it should not be an e-mail. I talk to people all the time who at work rely on e-mail for all forms of important communication, so they're using e-mail as their default. Here is the problem: e-mail may not always be the best solution for what it is you're trying to communicate. So you have to decide before you even create an e-mail or respond to one—is this the best format or venue for communicating this particular message? I also believe if you get into an e-mail exchange or you have to go back and forth with the other person multiple times, you're much better off picking up the phone to communicate with them in a two-way form, or to actually walk down the hallway and have a human discussion face to face. This will benefit you in two ways: 1) it will reduce the number of e-mails you are sending, and 2) it will give you less e-mails to organize and respond to.

### Idea #11—Block the box

I see far too many people who answer an e-mail, pick up the phone to make a phone call, answer another e-mail, make another phone call, go to a meeting, and then answer some more e-mails. I believe this is highly inefficient and ineffective. The best way to process your e-mail is to process it all at once if you can. What I recommend is creating blocks in your calendar that are set aside for all similar activities—blocks of time to answer e-mail, blocks of time to do project work, and blocks of time to do phone calls. By doing related activities at the same time, you can be much more efficient because you will be in the groove and in a rhythm without being interrupted.

### Idea #12—Turn down the noise

Almost all e-mail systems have an audible sound that is made when you have received a new message. This seems like a great idea on the surface because the new e-mail comes in and you hear a nice pleasant "ding" sound. You and I both know, however, that becomes extremely tempting; if you're in the middle of sending one e-mail and you hear that sound, you are tempted to delay the e-mail that you're working on to look at the new e-mail that you just received. I guess human beings are often like Pavlov's dog—the bell rings, and we feel we have to react. It's just like when the phone rings, you feel like you have to answer it. So one way to reduce your level of distraction is to turn down your notification sound.

### Idea #13—Let me be clear

One other technique which might help you be more organized and save time is to write your e-mails in a more organized fashion. First, make sure that you have a subject line which is very specific and addresses exactly what it is that you're writing about. For example, you may say, "Subject: Information about the proposal for the Wilson account." This allows anyone reading your e-mail to know exactly what the topic is before they read it. Secondly, keep your e-mails short and sweet, and instead of writing in long paragraphs, write in short bulleted points. Research has shown that when people are busy, e-mails that are written with short bullet points are much easier to read and understand and digest than trying to read through long drawn-out paragraphs to extract the important information. Tell the person you are sending the e-mail to exactly what it is you want them to do. For example, you could say, "I would like to have the preliminary numbers back to me by the end of Thursday at five o'clock." Far too many people send e-mails, and I'm not really sure why the e-mail was sent because they don't outline what it is they want me to do. Are they sending me the e-mail just as an FYI, do they want a decision, do they want an answer or an opinion, do they want a response, and when do they want me to get back to them by? By doing this you will be much more organized because you will get better and more complete responses from the people that you send e-mails to.

### Idea #14—Trash day

Even though it seems like a remarkably obvious suggestion, either at the beginning of each day or the end of each day you should take time to go through and delete items from your inbox. Following the three-step system that I outlined earlier in this chapter will help you decide what you want to do with each e-mail. If you do it at the end of the day, it gives you a fresh start the next day because you start with an inbox that is in control, perhaps almost nearly empty. If you do it at the beginning of the day you will have the same feeling because you will stary the day off on the right foot. The problem is most people wait way too long to delete items from their inbox. Don't do this to yourself because it creates a lot more time, work, effort, and energy to organize because there's just too much information in your inbox.

### Idea #15—It's in the script

One suggestion you might want to consider is to create specific scripts that you can use to respond to requests that you get repeatedly. If you find yourself constantly writing e-mail responses to a couple of very general questions that you are often getting, then take some time to write out the scripted responses that you can literally cut and paste and put into your e-mail to save you tons of time and effort.

### Idea #16—That's really curious

Sometimes you get an e-mail from someone about something that you find to be quite fascinating and in the future you may want to look into further, but it seems to kind of defy being put into a category. What you may want to think about is creating an individual folder that is just for things that you find curious, interesting, stimulating, or that you'd like to know more about in the future. That way you don't have to get rid of the e-mail or the link or the website; you can move it into a folder and look at it when you get a moment.

### Idea #17—Easy access

The other most important decision you need to make about your e-mail is to decide where you are going to access it, and how you're going to access it, and when you're going to access it. If you are like me, you are checking e-mail from work, from home, and from your phone. Some people are also checking e-mail from other electronic devices such as an iPad or a Kindle. So just make sure that if you're going to check any of your e-mail accounts that you have easy access from any of those devices so that you can read your e-mail wherever you happen to be.

## APPLICATIONS

The great thing today is that there are all kinds of applications you can find for your desktop, your iPad, or your phone. There are applications for note taking, applications for to-do lists, and applications for time tracking. My suggestion is to go on an online store on your phone or laptop and search for applications by category. There are many new ones coming out almost every day. Experiment and try to find any that may work for you.

When you think about applications and technology to increase your productivity, there are several categories that you probably want to look at in order to increase your productivity in those particular areas. The analogy that I use is it's kind of like having a bag of golf clubs—which club do you need for which shots? It would be smart to use a putter for putting, the driver for hitting your drive, and a sand wedge for your shots from the sand trap. It's the same with technology and applications—you should choose the right technology for the right reason and the right tool. As part of this discussion, I will not be making a distinction between applications and software that are available for your phone or for your laptop or other devices. Many applications and technologies are now available across all platforms; you just have to find out if the application you're looking for is available and which devices you could use it on.

## DOCUMENTS

There are many great tools that you can use for managing your documents. The great thing is you can use tools to manage documents for yourself individually; you can also use some collaborative tools to share documents with others. The key point with technology that you want to use for documents is to determine what it is you need *to do* with the technology. For example, there are several pieces of technology out there through which we can create a document and store it somewhere on the cloud until someone else can get the document, read it, review it, or even modify it. Some examples of these would be Google Docs, Microsoft Office 360, or Microsoft OneDrive. I guarantee you when you look up "document-management" you will find dozens or maybe even hundreds of different pieces of software that will help you manage documents; you just have to decide which one works best for you.

## STORAGE

In the complex times that we live in, it is often complicated when we create documents that contain large amounts of data, that contain video or audio files or that contain PowerPoints or other presentation types of media. One simple way to solve this is to use some type of cloud storage system. Two examples of this are Dropbox and also a program called Box. The best way to explain how these technologies work is they are basically like taking a file and storing it in a virtual warehouse, and then sending someone else the key to walk into the warehouse and pick up your file. On Dropbox, for example, you create a file and then send the link to someone else to their e-mail. They then follow the link and are able to open the document or file that you sent in order to access it. The reality is the main reason why these storage technologies exist is that many files are too large to e-mail and when you attempt to e-mail them the server tells you it's too large a file to send. I have found these technologies to be extremely useful, particularly when I was working on e-learning programs and needed to send other people large video files for them to review. I would simply send them a link and they would then go to Dropbox and download the MP4 file. I was amazed at how easy and efficient this was. You just need to decide which storage software technology would be best for you, and sometimes you may find that the company you work for already subscribes to those kinds of services. So find out from your IT department the ones your company might have. Also keep in mind that some IT departments will not allow you to download certain kinds of software without their permission, so you may wish to check with them first before doing so.

## NOTE TAKING

Some people like to take notes on an iPad, laptop, legal pad, in a journal, or actually in their paper time management system that they use. In my opinion there's no right or wrong answer; you may also want to consider using technology for taking notes. This can save time and energy and make you more productive because notes entered into technology usually do not get lost. There are some very interesting note-taking apps on the market such as Evernote, OneNote, NoteTaker, and Sticky Notes. The way most of the note-taking software works is you simply open up the application and make a quick note; in some applications you can cut and paste information into a document and then save it into a file. The one advantage of these applications is that they are cloud based, so if you can get a connection you can access your notes from anywhere in the world. You just need to decide how you want to take notes (do you want to use the analog approach or the digital approach?), and then you need to decide how you want the notes to be stored. No matter whether you use a manual method, where you're writing notes on paper, or an electronic method, where you're recording notes electronically, you still have to decide how your notes are going to be stored.

## PROJECT MANAGEMENT

In order to be productive, I highly recommend that you use some sort of project management system. In certain specific industries there may be proprietary project management software that your company has already purchased and is available to you. For example, if you're a construction manager and in the construction industry, there is proprietary software that you can use to manage a construction project. If you work for a company, your company may already have project management software that they subscribe to or have bought. The basic idea behind project software applications is to have everything in one spot as it relates to the managing of the projectwhile also being able to collaborate with all others who are working on the project at the same time. Some examples of these kinds of project management applications ares Trello and Basecamp. I believe that project management software makes you much more productive because it allows you to gather all your information in one place to track multiple items at once.

## TASK MANAGEMENT

You may want to organize your to-do list on a piece of paper, or you may decide to use technology for your to-do list or your task list. If you have an e-mail system at work, you may take a closer look and discover that within that e-mail system is also a calendar system and a task list system that you can use. So, for example, you can put something on a to-do list and list the date a week away, and it will then populate your to-do list seven days from then. If that is not available to you and you would like to use technology for your to-do list further, you can look at applications and technologies for keeping a task list. Some examples of these are Wunderlist and Any.do. These are just a few examples, but there are tons of them out there that you can take a look at and decide which one works for you in terms of helping make you more productive.

## GROUP COMMUNICATION

I have already mentioned group collaboration and project management tools such as Trello and Basecamp. In addition to those, you may also want to use some different tools to communicate with groups when you need to communicate with them live virtually (when you cannot be with them in person). Among such technologies are Google Hangouts, Skype, and Adobe Connect, just to name a few. I think one of the things that you want to think about is, do you want everyone to be able to see one another or not? Some programs allow you to put up Power-Point and documents and have the audio connection by phone or through a computer's microphone. In those systems, however, each person in the group cannot see each other; they can usually only see the host of that particular meeting if they have their webcam activated on the computer. So you need to ask yourself if it's important for the group to be able to see one another and if so, make that part of your criteria as you review different group communication tools and technologies.

## TRAVEL PRODUCTIVITY

There are many great technologies and software that will help you to be more productive when traveling, specifically those that organize the details and logistics of your travel. Obviously, one form of travel productivity is using online booking sites to book your flight, hotels, or rental cars. Some examples of this type of technology would be Expedia.com, Travelocity.com, Hotels.com. To organize the rest of your trip details, you can use many pieces of technology and applications that help you store data about your trip. Two examples of these would be TripIt and TripCase, and, for travel, particularly airline travel, SeatGuru. So try to figure out how you can use technology applications to make yourself less stressed and more productive.

## CONTACT MANAGEMENT

If you are extremely busy working and having a bunch of different tasks all at once—the big question is, where do you store all your contact information for all the people with whom you're in contact? These could be associates, colleagues, vendors, suppliers, or partners. Some people are replacing the old-fashioned address book with a piece of technology known as a contact management system. The idea behind contact management systems is that you can store all the data about a particular person and efficiently remind yourself of what you're supposed to follow up with them by e-mail or phone, or even when certain tasks are due to those particular people. Some examples of contact management systems are Salesforce, and EZ Contact Book. Many of these contact management systems also integrate with an e-learning system that makes communication easy to transfer and store between each system.

## TRACKING EXPENSES

If you are in the world of business, it is obviously important for you to track expenses, whether it is lunch with a client or a weeklong road trip. You can certainly track expenses on paper, but you may also want to look at different ways of tracking expenses with either a phone or laptop application. Some examples of expense tracking technology would be Expensify, Fresh-Books, and Hello Expense. Using expense tracking software or applications may save you time in having to record expenses and filling out expense reports and not being able to remember how much you spent.

## SAVING WEB CONTENT

I'm sure there are many times when you see on the Internet a specific website or story that you are interested in and would like to read further but do not have the time at that moment to read. There are several pieces of technology that you can use to set aside articles and websites that you want to read later. Obviously, one of the first approaches is to use the save function in your particular Web browser. Each one of them works differently. Most Web browsers do have the opportunity to create favorites to save that particular site to your favorites to read later. On your phone or laptop also, you can use software that captures the links to those articles so that you can read them later. One example of that would be Pocket, which helps you save the links and puts them into a folder for you to review when you have time.

## FINANCIAL

If you work for yourself and own your own business, then obviously you are going to need to track financial elements, and you're going to need to invoice customers and clients and do all the other bookwork that goes along with owning and running a business. You could ask your CPA to recommend a software technology. There are many popular ones out there such as QuickBooks and Freshen. One great advantage about many of the financial technologies that are out there is that they have reporting capabilities and you can share files with your accountant and have them modified and sent back to you.

## VOICE RECOGNITION

One idea that you might want to think about is the idea of using voice recognition software to increase your level of productivity for writing and sending e-mails. There are many different voice recognition technologies on the market, some examples being Dragon, Tazti, and TalkTyper. The way most voice recognition systems work is you buy or license the product, then once you receive it you have to train the software to recognize your vocal patterns. Once that is in place, which does not take very long, the software then literally types whatever you say. I have had a lot of experience with voice recognition software, and I find it to be a tremendously productive tool and about 95% accurate. This is a technology you may seriously want to consider in order to speed up the writing of documents, e-mails, and reports.

So those are some things to think about in terms of using technology in order to enhance and increase your productivity. The big question is, where do you find the technology that you're looking for? First, I think it is useful to do an online search for that particular software that you're looking for, which would then give you lots of choices. Secondly, you can go on your phone to your "marketplace" of whatever brand phone you have to download apps that are applicable to your phone. Third, if you work in a company you may want to talk to people in the IT department and ask them about specific software applications that apply to whatever you're trying to do.

After you find technology that you might be interested in, experiment with them to see what works for you and what doesn't, and constantly be on the lookout for new ideas and concepts.

Joseph B. Wirthlin once said, "Each minute is a little thing, and yet, with respect to our personal productivity, to manage the minute is the secret of success."

# WORK IT!

How do you feel about using technology to increase productivity?

_____

_____

_____

_____

What suggestions about e-mail did you find most helpful?

_____

_____

_____

_____

What is your biggest productivity challenge?

_____

_____

_____

_____

What technology may be helpful?

_____

_____

_____

_____

Why?

_____

What category of apps do you think may be most helpful?

Which ones do you plan on looking at first?

# CHAPTER TEN

## *JOLT #10*
# TAKE BREAKS TO BOOST PRODUCTIVITY

## THE POWER OF R&R: USING DOWNTIME TO INCREASE YOUR PRODUCTIVITY

*"But by taking the time away, getting myself off the treadmill, and just slowing down and learning, I felt I had so much more to give back. And maybe that was something that needed to happen for all of us."*
—LINDSEY BUCKINGHAM

As a professional speaker and book author, I often work with many companies across America every year. The thing that I find most fascinating about most companies, with very few exceptions, is that most people working in the office *do not take breaks* in the morning or in the afternoon. Most people who eat their lunch at work eat at their desk and work while they are eating their lunch.

So, in essence, people are working at work and *not taking breaks*. It's kind of funny because in the industrial age, people were automatically given a morning break, a lunch break, and an afternoon break, which were signaled by whistle. Somewhere along the way in the shift in culture from the industrial age to the information age, the idea of a break for the information worker went out the window.

Ironically, scientific research shows that when people take breaks they are much more productive and effective. In a study at Baylor University, Drs. Emily Hunter and Cindy Wu studied the break habits of close to one thousand workers. I'm sure that you will not be shocked to find out what they found. They found that taking a break in the morning, before lunch, was more effective at replenishing energy, concentration, and motivation. Workers who took breaks early in the day were more productive later in the day. No big surprise there.

So study after study after study indicates that people are much more effective when they take breaks, so why it that most people across the world are not doing so?

### Pressure

Many people that I talk to about taking breaks tell me that they are under a tremendous amount of pressure to produce, and they are working in companies that run very lean, and they are single-handedly doing two people's jobs. So they feel like they're under too much pressure already to get the work done, and so taking a break would be counterproductive.

### Perception

Many years ago when I worked in corporate America, I started at a new company. The one thing I noticed immediately is that no one on the team ever took a morning or afternoon break and that everyone on the team worked at their desk when they were eating lunch. So the perception in that department was that people really weren't allowed to take breaks and that people really weren't allowed to go out to lunch just to get away from work. Whether that perception was accurate or not is hard to say, but that was a perception. Nobody wanted to be perceived as lazy by taking a break. So there's a very strong message delivered in the culture that says that breaks are not something that "we do." That perception makes people afraid to buck the system or to go against the culture because they fear the implications of doing so.

### Not encouraged to

I recently read an article about W.L. Gore, where they made it a corporate policy that all employees were *required* to take morning breaks and lunch breaks and afternoon breaks. Even more importantly, they trained the managers to closely monitor team members and to insist that they take a break and to encourage them to do so. In many organizations, this is actually the opposite of what happens; employees are not encouraged to take breaks and are actually discouraged from taking a break, and there is an implied message that taking a break is not a good thing and that it is not productive.

### Perceived reward

In many organizations, it strikes me that there's a perception that the people who never take breaks, the people who work all weekend, the people who work on vacation, and the people who stay at work late are promoted and rewarded for their dedication and commitment, which involve certainly not taking breaks ever.

I meet people who brag about never using all their vacation days, and they are proud of that accomplishment.

### Guilt

Many people that I talk to tell me that they feel guilty if they take a break when other people continue working, or that their lousy manager makes them feel guilty for taking a break. Please do not feel guilty for taking a break. You're actually taking a break so you can be a more productive employee, not a less productive employee. Secondly, you actually are entitled to take a break, and if you're like most people, you've given a lot of time and a lot of effort to your company when you haven't been paid. When I worked in corporate America, there were many nights that I worked late, and there were many times when I came in and worked over the weekend because I was working on some project, so if you added up the number of hours that I voluntarily gave to the company, the hours were in the hundreds of thousands. So why would anyone feel guilty about taking a 15-minute break in the morning and a 15-minute break in the afternoon? Because they feel like they're not entitled to a break—but trust me, you are entitled and you should feel entitled. You work hard and you earned it.

## THE BREAK MANIFESTO

So the reality is that all scientific research shows that you are much more effective if you take breaks. These facts are inarguable and proven by tons of research over the last two decades. So if you want to truly be more productive, you need to start habitually taking breaks at work. Here are some ideas that you might want to incorporate in order to make sure that you are more productive.

### Take a morning break

If you have a time management system (paper or electronic), I want you literally to go into the system and plan your morning break. That's roughly somewhere halfway between when you start and when lunchtime is. When your system reminds you that it is 10:30—time to take a break—I want you to stop everything that you're doing (that is unless you are in the middle of a phone call) and take your break.

### Leave your work area

When you are taking a 15-minute break in the morning or in the afternoon, actually get up and leave the workspace to give yourself a mental and physical break. Go for a walk, go to another part of the building, go to the company cafeteria or anywhere else, but physically leave your work area and give your mind, your eyes, and your body a break from the work. I think you will find that when you actually do this, you'll come back to the work refreshed and more productive and efficient. I'm sure in the back of your mind you're probably thinking, "What will people think that I'm taking a break?" The way to stop worrying about what other people think about your taking a break is to realize that when you're more productive, they will realize that your taking a break actually had a positive impact, not a negative one.

### Take a lunch break

The same kind of rules apply when you're taking a lunch break. I want you to actually get up and leave your workspace and go eat lunch somewhere else, and I'm asking you *not to do any work* while you're at lunch. You can take 30 to 45 minutes for lunch and disconnect from work by eating lunch outside, in your company cafeteria, or anywhere else, but please, not at your desk. If you are worried about people wondering where you are at lunch, tell someone in your department that you are going to lunch, and within a few weeks people will get used to the idea that you're not working through lunch.

### Take an afternoon break

I know it sounds completely crazy (not really), but you should take an afternoon break somewhere halfway between when you come back from lunch and when you go home at the end of the day. If you take afternoon breaks, you will be much more productive when you come back to do the work.

## VACATION AND TIME AWAY

Sometimes when working on a project with a client, I will be asked to dial into a group conference call to talk to all the people involved with the project. One thing that happens often that I find appalling is that many times someone on the call is calling into the conference *from vacation*. During the call, there will be some background noise like seagulls or amusement park rides, and someone on the call will ask what the noise is. Someone on the call then proudly announces that they are calling in from the beach where they are on vacation with their family. So many people are working when they're on vacation, calling into conference calls, working on projects, returning phone calls, checking voice mail, and sending e-mails. When I ask people why they're doing this, they tell me that they feel pressured by the management of the company and their boss to produce even when they're on vacation. It is either an expected or an implied requirement. I personally think this is a terrible idea, as the idea of vacation is to *vacate* and to give your brain, your body, and your soul a break from the work. That's the right vacation, which is a reward for your mind, body, and soul.

Secondly, I believe that working while on vacation is extremely unfair to your family, including your spouse and your children, because you're not giving them your undivided attention, which is split between work and vacation. Look, your kids are only going to be 10 years old once. As much as our society believes that kids want things, what they really want is for you to spend time with them. Vacations are a chance to bond as a family and to create special memories that will last a lifetime. Don't ruin it by being on e-mail when your kids are swimming in the pool and want you to come in and swim with them.

So a legitimate question you may be asking is, how in the world are you going to be able to "get away with that" if you work for a company? (If you work for yourself, just tell yourself it is okay to go on vacation and not work.) Here are some strategies you may find helpful:

### *Try to contract with your boss*

If you have a good relationship with your boss, find an appropriate time to have a meeting with him and explain that you're going on vacation and will work twice as hard before you leave and twice as hard when you get back, but that you do not intend to do any work when you're on vacation. Then stick to your guns. When I was a vice president in corporate America, I had 16 people who reported to me. One of the key rules that I had for the people that reported to me was about vacation. I told them that when they were on vacation I did not want them to check e-mail, I did not want them to call and check voice mail, I did not want them on work-related conference calls, and I did not want them to work. I told them they were on vacation and that the idea of vacation was to vacate and to relax and spend time with friends and family. Lastly, I made them leave their work laptop with me, and they were not allowed to take it with them on their trip. People really appreciated this approach, and I found that they came back from vacation relaxed and refreshed and ready to be productive.

### Go somewhere where there's no signal

If the management in your company does not agree with your not working on vacation, then one simple approach is to literally go somewhere where there is no signal. There are ranches that advertise that they are technology free and therefore no signal is available there for your phone or your e-mail. I have stayed in the mountains and many places where as soon as I got to the location, the signal on my cell phone completely disappeared so I wasn't able to make any calls on my cell phone. So simply tell the people that work in the management of your company that you will be going to a place where you're not able to be reached. If your company is going to be demanding that you do work on vacation, then you need to come up with a counterstrategy to work against it. My other thought is that if you do great work the rest of the year, then it doesn't matter if you're not available for a week or two during the year.

### Slice up the day

While I'm certainly not advocating this approach, if you work for a company that absolutely will not allow you not to answer e-mails every day or not to respond to certain requests, then use a strategy I call "slicing up the day." The strategy is simply picking some time in the day (like early morning or late at night) and setting aside time to respond to e-mail after the children are asleep or before they get up. At least then you're having a minimal impact on your family by working on vacation. But I would honestly and passionately urge you to think about not taking this approach because it is not a vacation, but simply working from another place. Everyone needs a break, and if you do not take a break, it certainly will, at some point, have an impact on your health mentally and physically.

### Delegate

If you know you are going to be on vacation and you plan it well, you can try to arrange to delegate your roles and responsibilities to other people while you're gone. If you cross-train people to perform those functions when you're out, then they can fill in for you. In exchange, you can cross-train in their functions, and when they are out you can fill in for them. This also is usually pretty well received by management because they know that someone is going to be covering for you when you're out.

### Practice advanced planning

Talk with your family as early in the year as possible, and plan your vacations for the entire following year. Look at the calendar and, between you and your spouse, plan your vacations, long weekends, all your days off, and, if you have children, also take a look at the school calendars to make sure that there is no conflict. I find that, generally, when you practice advanced planning you can get your vacation times approved by your boss early and plan your vacations and let management get used to the idea that you're going to be away during those times. As those times rapidly approach, remind them that you're going to be on vacation.

## DRAWING THE LINE

I constantly meet people who tell me that their bosses expect them to answer phone calls at night, and sometimes even late at night. They tell me that their bosses expect them to answer e-mails at night and on weekends and holidays. Husbands and wives sometimes tell me that they have banned their spouse from having the phone in the bedroom at night because they are constantly checking it until midnight every night. I see couples out to dinner Friday or Saturday night, and one of them is still checking e-mails and voice mails on the phone that are obviously work related. I think that in order for you to be as productive as possible, you need to decide where to draw the line. Everyone needs downtime, everyone needs breaks, and no one can work 24/7. So here are some thoughts about drawing the line:

### Decide on the boundaries

Here is the question: At what time in the evening should you stop answering when people send you a text message or an e-mail? Is it at nine o'clock or at ten o'clock? I think it is time for you to start training people that you do not answer your e-mail on weekdays after a certain time of day, and you have to decide what the timeline is—perhaps after eight o'clock in the evening you no longer respond to e-mails. I understand there are sometimes emergencies, and that is a different story. There may be occasions in the world of business when something needs to be handled immediately, but that is the exception rather than the rule. When you don't answer an e-mail after eight o'clock and someone at work tells you, "Hey, I sent you an e-mail last night at 10, but you didn't respond!" just simply say, "I was already asleep."

You also need to know where the boundaries are in regard to when you're going to answer e-mails or text or phone calls on weekends. You may want to question whether you answer them at all. If you feel that you must answer them, then you need to decide again where the boundaries are. Sadly, I often see parents at their kids' sports events sitting in the stands answering e-mails instead of watching their kids play football. I see parents answering a work-related phone call at a family birthday party and having to walk out of the room to take the call. We need to start drawing the line and not answering the phone on weekends if we are at important family events. We need to draw the line and not answer e-mails, texts, and phone calls if it is too early in the day or too late in the day. Maybe you don't answer on Sundays at all. Just keep in mind that when you respond to the request you will set a precedent that says that they *will always* expect you to respond.

If you are in management, I think it is up to you to take a leadership role and to model the concept of work-life balance. This means not expecting people to answer their phones or e-mails on weekends or late at night. This means not expecting an instant response when they are at a family event. This means explaining to them that you want their off time to be off and that you want them to spend time with their family and not have to worry about responding to an e-mail. If you're in management you should understand that if you give people time off to recover and recuperate, they will be more productive. They will have more energy, a better family life, and a much higher level of morale.

## RECOVERY

I believe that in order to be as productive as possible, you really have to try to focus on recovery in between the times that you are working. I believe that recovery falls into six major areas:

- Sleep

- Love

- Family

- Social activities

- Health and exercise

- Recreation

### Sleep

I think most people in the world, particularly during the work week, stay up too late and get up too early and usually during the week are in some sort of sleep deficit. Most people will tell you they do not get enough sleep. While I am not suggesting that you should get eight hours of sleep every single night, because I don't know if that's realistic, I do think that if you get more sleep you will be more productive during the day, so you have to determine how much sleep you need to be productive. Of course, throughout history there have been famous people who bragged about the fact that they hardly ever slept, including Thomas Edison and Margaret Thatcher. Most researchers think that there is no magic number for the sleep every person needs. Some people are able to survive on three or four hours of sleep each night, but, generally speaking, researchers say that any number below seven hours a night tends to have a negative impact on healthy adults.

If you want to be more productive, I just want you to think about possibly getting a little more sleep each night. If that is not possible, then, as some sleep experts say, at least sleeping in one day of the weekend can help you try to catch up with sleep deprivation. Admittedly, this idea is controversial—some experts agree and some experts don't—so I would experiment with what works for you.

### Love

So what in the world is the word "love" doing in a book about productivity? If rest and relaxation make you more productive, I believe that rest and relaxation become that much more fulfilling if you can share them with someone that you love. Taking time off to go on vacation, to do a day trip, to take a long weekend is much more enjoyable if you have someone to share it with. I highly recommend planning one or two long weekends a year with your spouse to get away and have some down time alone as a couple.

If you are currently not in a relationship and don't have someone that you are in love with, then I suggest investing some of your time in joining a dating site in order to find someone to love and to spend time with.

### Family

When I speak to groups when I'm doing my keynotes, I often mention the phrase that people find amusing: "you have to prioritize, calendarize, and agendasize." I realize that some of these are not words, but I use them to illustrate a key point. There is no question that you have to work to make a living, to pay your bills, and to support the lifestyle that you choose. But sadly, we sometimes get so caught up in doing work that we forget to prioritize spending time with family, including our children, other family members, and, most importantly, our spouses. You should plan time for vacationing with the family, for special family events, and for spending time with your children in both planned time (meaning, time on the calendar) and spontaneous time (meaning, throwing the football with your son or daughter). What I find most interesting is that some of my daughter's fondest memories were not fancy vacations or elaborate trips; they were simply times when I stepped out into the front yard and threw the football around with her. Spending time with those you love rejuvenates and restores your batteries, making you more productive when you actually have to go back in to work.

### Social

If you are married or single, do you have a social life? Do you plan and participate in social events with friends or participate in community events? You have to determine how much you want to get involved with these types of activities, but it can be very helpful to rest and relax and to get away from the pressures and stress of every-day work life. Being around great friends boosts your self-esteem, because it makes you feel good about yourself and makes them feel good about you. My wife's best friend, Julie, lives in another state, but we try to plan to see her and her husband a few times each year. My best friend, Dave, also lives in another state, but we make time several times a year to get together with him and his wife. We have several sets of friends that we make sure to do this with each year.

### Health and exercise

I see lots of studies reporting that only about 16% of the population works out on a regular and consistent basis. I want you to really consider adding exercise at least a few times a week into the routine of your busy life. There is one main reason why you should do that—it would dramatically increase your energy level, which will dramatically increase your productivity.

Last week I traveled to three different cities to speak to different groups. On Tuesday, I was in Maryland and did a full-day training program from nine o'clock until four o'clock. I then drove from Maryland to the Philadelphia Airport, then flew from Philadelphia to Milwaukee, Wisconsin, landed there at around 9:30 at night, rented a car, and drove two hours to my hotel. On Wednesday, I conducted a full-day training program from 9:00 to 4:00, and then drove two hours back to the Milwaukee Airport, where I flew from Milwaukee to Chicago, and then from Chicago to Dallas, Texas. I landed around twelve o'clock at night and then took a car service from the airport to my hotel. The next day I did a keynote address at a conference from nine o'clock to ten o'clock and then jumped on a plane to fly back home to Philadelphia. Having a schedule like this over a three-day time period requires a great deal of energy and stamina. I would not be able to do this if I were not healthy and if I were not very careful about my nutrition.

If you want to be productive, there are two things that can make an immediate impact on your productivity. First, try to get to your ideal weight, because if you're carrying around extra weight, that will make you more tired and less productive. I know that you already know this, but I'm sure in some ways you've never thought about it being linked to productivity. Secondly, I would strongly recommend that you get on a regular and consistent exercise program. Please keep in mind that an exercise program does not have to mean anything extreme; even just going for a walk three times a week can make a big difference. It's just something I would like you to give deep thought to. Not only will it make you more productive, it will make your life last longer.

## Recreation

What I mean when I'm talking about recreation are sports and hobbies that help you get away from your normal activities and make you feel refreshed. Most recently, when speaking to a group, I asked everyone in the audience what the one activity was in terms of recreation that really recharged their batteries. When I called on one woman, she said that "being outside hiking or walking really helped her to de-stress." When I asked what it did for her, she said, "It restores my soul." When I asked her how often she was able to hike or walk, her answer was "never." When I asked her why, she said that she was too busy, working full-time and serving all of her roles as a wife, a mother, a daughter, and running a household. I was fascinated that she just did not have time to restore her soul. So for you, what are the activities that restore your soul?

When I see the word *recreation*, I actually see it as two words, re-creation! For too often when we become adults and we get busy, and we get serious, and we get mature, we often give up hobbies and activities that bring us joy. Maybe you love playing basketball or playing the drums or bird-watching or ballroom dancing or bowling. What I think you should do is set for yourself a goal of trying to mix in some of the things that bring you joy every week in terms of recreation, even if it's only for 30 minutes. In the ideal world, it would be something that your family enjoys as well, and you could do it together.

If you focus on making sure that you calendarize and prioritize the rest and relaxation, I guarantee you that when you go back to work you will be massively more productive.

> *"My ideal relaxation is working on upholstery. I*
> *spend hours in junk shops buying furniture. I do all*
> *the upholstery work myself, and it's like therapy."*
> —Pamela Anderson

# WORK IT!

How often do you take breaks at work?

_____

_____

_____

_____

If you don't take breaks, why not?

_____

_____

_____

_____

What would be the benefit if you took breaks?

_____

_____

_____

_____

Do you set limits on when you answer work e-mails or calls at home?

_____

_____

_____

Why would this be important?

_____

_____

_____

_____

Do you work on vacation?

_____

_____

_____

_____

Where would you rank yourself in terms of overall health, diet, and exercise?

_____

_____

_____

_____

Which area would you want to improve?

_____

_____

_____

_____

# CHAPTER ELEVEN

# FOLLOW THE LAW: THE 10 MOST POWERFUL PRINCIPLES OF PRODUCTIVITY

*"The bottom line is, when people are crystal clear
about the most important priorities of the organization
and team they work with and prioritize their
work around those top priorities, not only are they
many times more productive, they discover they
have the time they need to have a whole life."*
—STEPHEN COVEY

Here is what I believe are the core principles of productivity:

## PRINCIPLE #1: KNOW WHAT YOU WANT

I meet so many people in my career, speaking and executive coaching, who have sadly never made the time to really, totally, and completely think about what they want in their lives personally and professionally. It's almost as if they're not living their life on purpose, but living it accidentally. So the question I always ask is, if you don't know what you want, how will you know when you get it? Secondly, if you don't know what you want, be very careful because you may get what you don't want. Sometimes I see people achieve something and yet are miserable because it turns out that's not really what they wanted. To be productive, you must decide what it is that you want, and the only way to do that is to write down your goals, which will put you in the 3% of the population that is the most successful.

## PRINCIPLE #2: TRACK YOUR TIME

As far as I know, every person gets 24 hours in the day. Have you ever noticed, some people seem to squeeze more out of that day than others? I think that one of their secrets is they are very cognizant and aware of how they spend their time. They use some sort of time management system to track every minute of the day and how they spend it. Just like people who are financially successful have a financial budget, people who are successful and productive have a time budget, and they know exactly how they're going to spend it before it happens.

## PRINCIPLE #3: EVALUATE AND REEVALUATE

Socrates once said, "The unexamined life is not worth living." A lot of people that I meet across the world are living not examined lives but unexamined lives. One of the ways of being more productive is to constantly evaluate what you're doing and how you are doing it and try to figure out better ways to go about it. Right now the term "life hacking" is a very popular term, and I think it's actually a good one. The idea is to always be looking at your life personally and professionally and trying to figure out how to make it better, and using different tools and techniques in order to do it. Three to four times a year you should evaluate where you are personally and professionally and take a hard look at your goals and your progress.

## PRINCIPLE #4: WRITE IT DOWN

There is a ton of research to indicate that writing things down increases creativity, clarifies thinking processes, and allows you to think more clearly, deeply, and effectively. Some creativity experts refer to this as "displayed thinking." So it does not matter to me what format you use, whether it is on paper or electronically. I just want you to take some time to write down your goals and objectives so you can see them visually. As Summer Sanders once said, "If you write something down on paper, it becomes an actual goal. Before you write it down, it's a thought, a dream that may or may not get done."

## PRINCIPLE #5: STUDY/READ

I have not only written 20 books, but I also read a lot of books. So make sure to set aside some time every week to read articles from different websites, to read magazine articles that you find interesting or stimulating, and to read books to learn. Most people whom I meet who are highly successful always have some nonfiction book that they're in the middle of reading and that they find stimulating or thought provoking. I strongly suggest that you spend the majority of your reading time not reading fiction but reading nonfiction. Why do I say that? To use an analogy, I think that fiction is cotton candy for the mind and nonfiction, filet mignon. I am not saying you can't read fiction ever but that you should try to limit it to maybe a few fiction books a year. Pick any nonfiction category, whether it's self-improvement, biography, history, or how to; I just want you to pick a category, pick up a book, and start reading. I guarantee you any nonfiction you read will help expand your horizons and make you smarter, and when you're smarter, you are more productive.

## PRINCIPLE #6: TAKE TIME OFF

As outlined in the last chapter, it is very important to take time off to be the best you possible and to be more productive when you go back to work. I think time off should be a scheduled calendar priority, which includes vacations, long weekends, and holidays.

## PRINCIPLE #7: STOP TIME WASTERS

Everyone has in their day done certain things that we refer to as "time wasters": they may be surfing the Internet, spending time on Facebook, or maybe watching hours and hours of television. Please don't get me wrong—it's certainly okay to have some downtime to relax—that is not the issue—the issue is when we spend way too much time on time wasters and not enough time on the things that really matter. So carefully evaluate how much time you spend on those activities per week to try to minimize those numbers and spend time on more valuable endeavors such as reading or studying.

## PRINCIPLE #8: STAY FOCUSED

One of the challenges in today's world is staying focused when there are so many things to distract you, between your phone actually ringing, a text message dinging, e-mails clinging, and the person in your office asking if you have a minute. With today's meetings and projects and travel you have a big mess of the schedule. So it becomes even more important to have laser focus to set aside certain blocks of time just to work on the things that are important, and those times need to be uninter-ruptible. If you have to hide in a conference room, if you have to close the door and turn off the phone and turn away from your computer screen, whatever you need to do to stay focused, that's what you have to do.

## PRINCIPLE #9: TAKE CARE OF YOUR MOST VALUABLE ASSET—YOURSELF

In order to be most productive, you have to start thinking about taking care of yourself mentally, physically, and nutrition-ally. The more you can do that, the more you can be the best person for you and your family.

## PRINCIPLE #10: LIVE LIFE TO YOUR FULL POTENTIAL

If I was going to make a blanket statement about most people I meet across the world, I would say that most people that I meet are living life below their potential. Then you ask yourself, *are you living to your full potential*? If you looked at every area of your life and ranked each on a scale of 1 to 10, would you give every one of them a 9 or 10? I want you to live your best life possible, in a way that ensures that you live up to the talents and gifts that you have, and the life of maximum potential happi-ness, wealth, and success. One of the ways to do that is to be more productive.

**The rest is up to you.**

I think that Anne Frank said it best:

> *"Everyone has inside of him a piece of good news.*
> *The good news is that you don't know how great*
> *you can be! How much you can love! What you*
> *can accomplish! And what your potential is!"*
> —ANNE FRANK

# ABOUT THE AUTHOR

 Hi, I'm Shawn Doyle, CSP. It's nice to meet you! I am a certified professional speaker with the CSP designation. I'm sure you have heard of board-certified surgeons—I am a board-certified speaker. Only 3 percent of speakers in the world have this designation, so I am very proud of that and it is a mark of quality for you. I am also a certified corporate coach. My life passion is to make a positive difference in people's lives by helping them live to their full potential both at work and at home as people go through something called life.

I have spent almost three decades in the world of personal and professional development, and from 2000 to 2003 I co-founded Corporate University for Comcast where I was Vice President of Learning and Development. I have many amazing clients, some of which include Pfizer, Zippo, Comcast, Lockheed Martin, NBC, Aberdeen Proving Ground, Guidepost, ABC, Disney, Kraft, the U.S. Marines, Charter, TheLadders, and IBM.

I am known for my thought-provoking, fun, and highly interactive training programs and keynotes. That means you will get the results you are looking for and I guarantee it. The biggest compliment I get is being asked to come back again and again to work with my clients.

I am the author of 20 books, some of which include: *The 10 Foundations of Motivation* (iUniverse), *Sales Science* (Café Press),

*The Manager's Pocket Guide to Motivating Employees* (HRD Press), *The Manager's Pocket Guide to Training* (HRD Press), *Juiced!—How to Be More Creative in Business and in Life!* (Café Press), as well as *2 Months to Motivation!* (Anfang Jeztz Publishing), *Jumpstart Your Motivation* (Sound Wisdom), *The Soul Survivor* (Destiny Image), *Jumpstart Your Leadership* (Sound Wisdom, 2013), *Jumpstart Your Creativity* (Sound Wisdom, 2013), *The Sun Still Rises* (Sound Wisdom, 2014), *Jumpstart Your Customer Service* (Sound Wisdom, 2014), *Jumpstart Your Business* (Sound Wisdom, 2015), and *Jumpstart Your Networking* (Sound Wisdom, 2016).

I am a contributing writer for The Huffington Post, Entrepreneur, Addicted2Success, Lifehack, and The Good Men Project.

Four of my books are now beirachang translated into ten languages and are being distributed and sold in India, Malaysia, Singapore, China, and Quebec, Canada. I live in the scenic rolling hills of southwestern Pennsylvania made famous by Andrew Wyeth's paintings. I share my life with an amazing, wonderful wife and three crazy cats.

Contact me at:

www.shawndoylemotivates.com.

610-857-4742

## CONTACT SHAWN DOYLE, CSP

We would love to help you or your organization. Please contact us to learn more about:

- Keynote speeches for your meetings

- Training

- Executive coaching

- Life coaching

- Consulting

- Brainstorming